The Best Kept Secret

The Best Kept Secret

Single Black Fathers

Roberta L. Coles

ROWMAN & LITTLEFIELD PUBLISHERS, INC.
Lanham • Boulder • New York • Toronto • Plymouth, UK

ROWMAN & LITTLEFIELD PUBLISHERS, INC.

Published in the United States of America
by Rowman & Littlefield Publishers, Inc.
A wholly owned subsidiary of The Rowman & Littlefield Publishing Group, Inc.
4501 Forbes Boulevard, Suite 200, Lanham, Maryland 20706
www.rowmanlittlefield.com

Estover Road
Plymouth PL6 7PY
United Kingdom

British Library Cataloguing in Publication Information Available

Library of Congress Cataloging-in-Publication Data:

Coles, Roberta L.
  The best kept secret: single black fathers / Roberta L. Coles.
      p. cm.
  Includes bibliographical references and index.
  ISBN-13: 978-0-7425-6425-1 (cloth : alk. paper)
  ISBN-10: 0-7425-6425-8 (cloth : alk. paper)
  ISBN-13: 978-0-7425-6612-5 (electronic)
  ISBN-10: 0-7425-6612-9 (electronic)
  1. African American single fathers. 2. African American single fathers—Psychology.
3. Child rearing—United States. 4. Parenting—United States. 5. African American
families—Social conditions. I. Title.
  HQ759.915.C65 2009
  306.874'2208996073—dc22   2008037890

Printed in the United States of America

∞™ The paper used in this publication meets the minimum requirements of
American National Standard for Information Sciences—Permanence of Paper
for Printed Library Materials, ANSI/NISO Z39.48-1992.

To Robin, who inspired this study,
and to his son, Kellen.
Robin, you made the cliché—only the good
die young—too painfully true.

Contents

Acknowledgments

I am grateful to the reviewers for their insightful comments, to my colleague Charles Green for his constant encouragement to "hang in there," to my daughters, Claudia and Sage, for listening to me recount these fathers' stories. But my deepest appreciation goes, foremost, to the fathers embodied within the pages of this book, who welcomed me into their homes, opened their hearts, and gave me insight into their minds and lives and an understanding of a little-appreciated facet of American fatherhood—black single custodial fathers.

❧❧

CHAPTER ONE

Introducing a New Concept
Single Black Custodial Fathers

Rubin grew up in a house of women, three sisters and a single mom who worked two jobs. He saw his father twice during his life, the second time being his dad's funeral. Rubin describes his dad as a "street person," an artistic man who never found a productive outlet. Himself a "renaissance man," Rubin served in the military and traveled overseas. He reads widely, speaks philosophically, acts in local theater, and is good-looking enough to model. At the age of thirty, Rubin married a seventeen-year-old woman who, eight years later, sought a divorce because she needed to "find herself." By mutual agreement, Rubin took sole custody of their son and maintained their recently purchased home because he wanted to rear his son in a neighborhood with a higher rate of home ownership. At the time of the interview, he was employed as a paraprofessional in the city's public school system, but to make extra money he also worked as an assistant building manager for the school's sports games. For our interview, I sat at the dining table in his brick bungalow eating the German chocolate cake he baked that morning. It was a rainy day, and during my visit, Rubin had to place buckets under a couple roof leaks near the living room's bay window. Upstairs, his ten-year-old son, Kyle, played with his cousin, until they took a break to say hello and get their share of the cake. I asked Kyle to play something on his saxophone, but he was too shy to do so. Kyle's mother is a police officer and was the only mother among the fathers interviewed to pay regular child support.

Raymond is the gay son of a Pentecostal minister. Three years prior to our interview, he had been working for the governor's office in a western state when his biological clock started ticking. Raymond had hoped to one day establish a lifelong partnership that would lead to a parenting arrangement, but so far that hadn't happened, and he began to wonder whether he would ever experience the joy of rearing children. Rather than waiting for the elusive "right" time, Raymond began looking into adoption on his own. Shortly, child services sent him the file of a four-year-old boy who had already been in nine foster homes. Raymond knew immediately that this was the child for him. In fact, he was enamored with and eager for the parenting challenge. But a few months later, when the day-to-day parenting of a preschooler with emotional and behavioral problems became reality, Raymond was shocked. Within the year, Raymond and his son, Tommy, moved to the capital city of a Midwestern state to secure good schools and an environment conducive to child rearing. One Good Friday evening, sitting at an unsteady kitchen table, I interviewed Raymond in their simply furnished two-bedroom apartment that was full of photos of friends and family. Tommy, now six and a first grader at a local public school, played in his bedroom until his curiosity got the best of him. Then he came out to show me some of his toys and ask questions. During our talk, Tommy's babysitter and her daughter dropped by to give him an Easter basket. Giving Tommy a hug and kiss, she warned him not to eat all the candy at once. Having survived the initial shock of instant parenting, Raymond said he was considering adopting another child.

Jay's parents separated when he was young. His father preferred the rural life in Virginia, while his mom preferred the city life of Philadelphia. Jay and his eight siblings spent the school year with his mom and summer with Dad. But his parents remained lifelong friends, and his father visited Philadelphia frequently, supplying them with much of the meat from his hunting. When Jay married his wife in his early thirties, he had not wanted children. He and his wife both had good jobs and were making a good income, which they invested wisely. However, after a few years, his wife persuaded him to have children; one by one, they had two sons and then a daughter. Within a few months of their daughter's birth, Jay's wife died unexpectedly of a brain aneurysm. Jay attempted to continue working for a while but his distraction caused him to make a dangerous mistake on the job. He was also unhappy with the nannies he hired to care for his children, especially his second son who had been born prematurely and needed additional in-home medical care the first few years of his life. So Jay quit his job and lived on their investments and worked part-time. He held his sons back in school a year so that they could adjust better to their mother's death, and then he finally moved to a smaller town in a Midwestern state, where he hoped it would be easier to rear children safely. At the time of the interview, Jay is in his late fifties. Recovering from recent knee surgery, he arrives at our interview in a local coffee shop (he says his house was "too messy") using a cane. Otherwise he assures me he's in excellent shape. Jay quickly informs me that he would prefer to be called American, rather than African American or black. He works part-time for a national parcel delivery service and on the side is developing his own karaoke business, specializing in 1950s doo-wop music. After fifteen years of sole custody, his oldest son, Rory, attends a local technical college and had just moved back in to help Jay through the surgery recovery. Just recently, his second son, Josh, left home without any notice, and Jay said most of the gray hairs on his head sprang from this concern. He knew his son was alive but did not understand why he had left. His daughter, Brie, was now in high school.

What do these men have in common? They are all African American men. They are all single, custodial fathers, loving and parenting their children on their own. And they apparently comprise a demographic that has remained imperceptible in the recent public debate over black fatherhood. In his 2008 presidential campaign, Barack Obama wanted to be clear where he stood on the politicization of family values: "Too many black fathers . . . have abandoned their responsibilities, acting like boys instead of men. And the foundations of our families are weaker because of it" (Eilperin 2008). Several weeks later, the Rev. Jesse Jackson chastised Obama for ignoring the structural impediments to quality fathering that black men face. He explained (Zeleny 2008), "My appeal was for the moral content of [Obama's] message to not only deal with the personal and moral responsibility of black males, but to deal with the collective moral responsibility of government and the public policy which would be a corrective action for the lack of good choices that often led to their irresponsibility." The Obama-Jackson tiff epitomizes the oversimplified dichotomous, either-or, approach taken toward social problems, which are too often posed as solely the results of poor individual choices *or* (sometimes intentional) systemic barriers. But worse yet, in the scurry to reprimand and find blame, conscientious black fathers have been erased, treated as nonexistent or as if their existence might endanger the monolithic picture of the irresponsible black father.

To be sure, there are irresponsible fathers, African American and otherwise. And African American fathers represent a disproportionate share of them if irresponsibility is defined by nonresidence with the child, but let's place them in a larger context. Over the past half century, life expectancy increased and fertility declined, marriage has been postponed and cohabitation has increased. Consequently, some observers have suggested that marriage and parenting now occupy a quantitatively smaller proportion of everyone's life, whether male or female and across races. For men, in particular, living with their children is a diminishing feature of adulthood (Eggebeen 2002).

Fatherhood—defined as the state of *parenting* children, not merely conceiving them—has evolved in what might appear contradictory directions.

From the "happy days" of the married, instrumentally providing father who was paradoxically present in the home yet distant from the everyday aspects of parenting, contemporary fatherhood has separated that paradox in two directions. Although I would not go quite this far, one scholar (Forste 2002) has argued that fathers have split into two distinct categories of "good dads" and "bad dads." On one end of the spectrum, some men are more present in parenting than ever before, diving into fatherhood with gusto. As industrial jobs shrank and women inundated colleges and workplaces with calls for equality, demands for qualitatively better fathering to compensate for women's reduction in at-home time pulled men more deeply into the father role. Moreover, the decline in fertility rates has enabled both parents to invest more time, money, and emotion in each child.

On the other end of the spectrum, some fathers are distanced from parenting through divorce and increased nonmarital births. Fathering-in-residence has become a path less trodden. With the rise in nonmarital births and single-mother households, men have a greater chance of not even knowing they are fathers. And despite improvements that incorporate fathers in childbirth, social policy often still treats fathers only as financial providers, and lingering stereotypes about women's inherent ability to parent frequently lead to men being viewed as a disposable parent (Leite 2007).

These trends in increased divorce, marriage postponement, and cohabitation, combined with earlier sexual activity and higher nonmarital birthrates have occurred at higher rates for African Americans and created a noticeable disjuncture between biological fatherhood and parenting. Consequently, a steep decline in the percent of black children living in married-couple households has occurred. Until 1980 the majority of African American children lived with both parents, but a steady decline over two decades has put that number at 35 percent in 2006 (U.S. Census Bureau 2007b). Now 51 percent of black children live with mothers only, a trend accompanied by a concomitant image that those children's fathers are absent from the children's lives. While many fathers do disappear from their children's lives, particularly over time and particularly poor fathers, we nevertheless now know that a substantial minority of nonresident fathers continue to be involved to one degree or another in their children's lives.

Although findings are mixed, some quantitative and qualitative studies find that of men who become fathers through nonmarital births, black men are least likely (compared with white and Hispanic fathers) to marry or cohabit with the mother (Lerman and Sorensen 2000; Mott 1990). Yet some studies also suggested that black nonresident fathers tend to maintain their level of involvement over time better than do white and Hispanic nonresident fathers (Seltzer 1991; Stier and Tienda 1993; Coley and Chase-Lansdale 2000; Danziger and Radin 1990; Taylor et al. 1990; Wattenberg 1993), although in most cases involvement declines over time. Carlson and McLanahan's (2002) figures indicated that only 37 percent of black unmarried fathers were cohabiting (compared to 66 percent of white fathers and 59 percent of Hispanic), but 44 percent of unmarried black nonresident fathers were regularly visiting their children, while only 17 percent of white and 26 percent of Hispanic nonresident fathers were visiting. Recent research on fragile families by McLanahan, Garfinkel, Reichman, and Teitler (2001) investigated financial and nonfinancial support from young nonresident African American fathers at their first child's birth. The majority of them had contributed support during the pregnancy, visited at the hospital, declared paternity, and intended to remain involved. Similarly, Roy's (1999) study of low-income, nonresident black fathers in Chicago found that fathers contributed to their children in ways (such as caretaking and in-kind support) not captured or appreciated by formal surveys and government services (See also Pirog-Good 1993). Smith et al. (2005) used longitudinal data to track young African American fathers' involvement with their eldest biological child. They found that black men did not differ significantly from young fathers of other races in their contact with and support provided to their child.

Much research and public monies have gone into investigating these single mothers and the nonresident fathers, attempting to measure the impact on their children (see for instance, Coley 1998; Demo and Cox 2000; Marsiglio et al. 2000; Menning 2002) and to reduce the numbers of nonresident fathers and children. Although the government's campaign to stimulate responsible fatherhood includes a broad array of initiatives (see www.fatherhood.hhs.gov), at the top of the list are policies aimed at shrinking the public costs of single parenting by securing child support payments or marriage among unmarried couples with children. In conjunction with the 1990s federal welfare reform package titled the Personal Responsibility and Work Opportunity Reconciliation Act, many states have instituted policies designed to increase the costs of single parenting to mothers through work requirements, limited eligibility, and lower benefits and to fathers through increased paternity establishment and child support enforcement (Plotnick et al. 2004). In addition, many states have promoted policies to encourage marriage, particularly among low-income populations (Ooms, Bouchet, and Parke 2004). It is presumed that such policies will reduce nonmarital childbearing, cut the number of single-parent families, and reduce the welfare rolls (Gennetian and Knox 2004; Lichter, Graefe, and Brown 2003). These will be discussed more in chapter 7, but my point here is that these monies, scholarly research, and public debate have nearly entirely focused on non-custodial fathers or so-called "irresponsible fathers," for which black fathers have become the poster child. Consequently, this has resulted in an ironic situation—absent black dads are very present in the cultural mind-set while present dads are essentially absent.

Without trivializing the potential negative outcomes for children whose fathers are absent from the home and uninvolved, or being indifferent to the pain of rejection that many of those children feel (Hunter et al. 2006; Matthews-Armstead n.d.; Barras 2000; Datcher 2001), I hope with this book to draw attention to the relatively small but persistent existence of black single custodial fathers, men who are present and involved with their children directly, rather than mediated by marriage. As shown in table 1.A, male-headed households[1] with children represented about 3.5 percent of all black households in 2000. This was nearly twice that of white male-headed households with children, which was 1.9 percent.[2] In addition, because these households often hold more than one child, they represent a slightly larger percentage of children. From the children's perspective, shown in table 1.B, about 4.8 percent of black children were living in a father-only household in 2006, just slightly higher than the 4.6 percent of white children who were living in father-only households. While these are not large percentages, they represent a fairly steady increase over the past few decades. For instance, in 1970, 2.3 percent of all black children lived with their fathers only, while .9 percent of all white children lived in father-only households (U.S. Census Bureau 2004). Also, because these are point-in-time surveys, these percent-

Table 1.A.   Family and Nonfamily Households Total and by Race, 2000

| | # of all Households | % of all households that were family | | | | | | | % of all households that were nonfamily | | |
		Family total	MC	MC w/c	Fehh total	Fehh w/c	Mhh total	Mhh w/c	Total	Live alone	2 or more
Non-Hispanic Black	11,862.087	67.8	31.3	17.9	30.8	23.4	5.7	3.5	32.2	27.1	5.1
Non-Hispanic White	79,093,136	66.5	54.3	23.8	8.8	5.5	3.4	1.9	33.5	27.3	6.2

MC = Married Couple
MC w/c = Married Couples with children 17 and under
Fehh = Female-headed household
Fehh w/c = Female-headed household with children 17 and under
Mhh = Male-headed household
Mhh w/c = Male-headed household with children 17 and under
Source: U.S. Census Bureau (2000).

Table 1.B.   Living Arrangements of Children under 18 Years, 2006

	Total # of children	% Living with both parents	% Living with mother only	% Living with father only	% Living with neither parent
Black Children	11,225	34.6	51.2	4.8	9.4
White Children	56,332	74	18	4.6	3.6

Source: U.S. Census Bureau (2007b, 2007c).

ages probably underestimate the percentages of children who ever live in a father-only household.

Not only have most studies on black fathering concentrated on absent/nonresident fathers, but they also have focused on low-income and/or teen fathers (Rivara, Sweeney, and Henderson, 1986,1987; Robinson 1988; Robinson and Barrett 1986; Savage 1987) and depended primarily on mothers' (or secondarily children's) reports (Ohalete 2007). Very little consideration has been given to fathers' own accounts of the fathering experience or to fathers who are parenting successfully (Ohalete 2007; Eggebeen 2002).

Until I started my research (Coles 2001a, 2001b, 2002, 2003), there was not one article on black single custodial fathers (since then there are two other qualitative studies that I'm aware of—Hamer and Marchioro 2002; Green, n.d.). Even some of the most recent additions to the literature on fatherhood by some of the leading scholars on fatherhood have neglected this population. For instance, Connor and White's 2006 edited volume, *Black Fathers: An Invisible Presence in America*, includes articles on married fathers, nonresident fathers, and father figures, but none on single custodial fathers. Ron Mincy's 2006 volume, *Black Males Left Behind*, included a couple chapters on black fathers, but these were poor and nonresident fathers. And in Marsiglio, Roy, and Fox's 2005 *Situated Fathering: A Focus on Physical and Social Spaces*, black fathers, also nonresident, were featured only in the chapter on responsible fatherhood programs.

This dearth of research on black single fathers is in part due to their relatively small numbers in the population (3.5 percent of 12 million black households is still fewer than 1.9 percent of 80 million white households), and they are less easy to access by white researchers, who still predominate in the academy. Also, the greatest nonresponse rate to surveys is found among never-married men, particularly low-income men (McLananhan et al. 2001; Bachu 1996; Lerman 1993). Moreover, Hatchett et al. (2000) and Ohalete (2007) suggest that historical misuse of African American respondents in some government and/or scholarly research, such as the Tuskegee experiment, the Moynihan report, and *The Bell Curve*, have exacerbated a distrust of research among African Americans as well. Finally, one can't help but wonder if spotlighting black men who father full-time of their own accord might contradict or threaten the research, programs, and policies oriented toward those who study, monitor, or work with nonresident fathers. In any case, I hope to begin to fill the gap in the literature with this narrative accounting of the parenting choices and experiences of twenty African American single custodial fathers.

A History of Studies on Single Fatherhood

A handful of studies on single white custodial fathers have been conducted, but a main question driving the studies of white single custodial fathers, which were mostly conducted in the late 1970s throughout the 1980s, is what factors made these fathers more likely than other fathers to take custody. Most of the studies looked at income, marital status, the degree of prior involvement, and the gender of the children as possible explanatory factors.

Research has found that white single custodial fathers tend to have a higher income and more full-time employment and rely less on social welfare than do single mothers and, frequently, single men (Christoffersen 1998; Chang and Deinard 1982; Dowd 1997; Downey 1994; Eggebeen, Snyder, and Manning 1996; Gersick 1979; Greif 1985, 1990; Guttman 1982; Hanson 1985, 1986, 1988; Meyer and Garasky 1993; Orthner, Brown, and Ferguson 1976; Risman 1986; Santrock and Warshak 1979). For instance, Greif and DeMaris (1989) surveyed 117 single white fathers, and they found that the average income was $7,000 more than the average income for single white men as a group. Meyer and Garasky's 1993 study of Current Population Survey data found that custodial dads had an income 187 percent greater than that of custodial moms. The fathers in this study similarly exhibited higher than average income and employment than that found among black single mothers and black single men. In 2000, the median household income among African Americans was $29,470 (DeNavas-Walt and Cleveland 2002) and about 15 percent of African American adult men had attained a college degree (U.S. Census Bureau 2003). But, as illustrated in table 1.C, more than half of this study's fathers had at least some college education, and more than 40 percent were making over $35,000 a year. However, even those fathers who were currently making a good salary had little to no wealth to rely on, about a third were working multiple jobs, and in a couple cases their jobs were insecure.

Table 1.C. Demographic Characteristics of the Study Fathers, by Number and Percent, at Time of Interviews

Age	#	%	Education	#	%	Income	#	%
20s or less	3	15	High school	7	35	Less than $15,000	3	15
30s	8	40	AA or some college	2	10	$15,000–24,999	3	15
40s	4	20	Bachelor's degree	8	40	$25,000–34,999	6	30
50s or more	5	25	Graduate degree	3	15	$35,000–49,999	2	10
						$50,000 or more	6	30

Several researchers (Clarke, Cooksey, and Verropoulou 1998; Furstenberg and Harris 1993; Seltzer 1991) have found that marital status at the time of the birth of a child is associated with the degree of father involvement (of both nonresident and custodial fathers). Nonresident fathers tend to be more involved over the long term if they were previously married to the mother (Furstenberg and Harris 1993; Lerman 1993). Likewise, studies of single custodial fathers, which are again largely based on white men, have found the majority of them to be divorced rather than never married. However, this was not true for the respondents in this study, nor is it true for black custodial fathers nationwide.

As shown in table 1.D, whereas the largest portion of white single fathers is divorced fathers, the largest portion—indeed the majority—of black single custodial fathers is "never married." This would be congruent with Clarke et al.'s 1998 study that found that black fathers' residence with their children was less affected by their relationship status with the mother at birth than was that of white or Hispanic fathers. Nevertheless, it is probable that divorced black fathers have a higher *rate* of subsequently taking custody than do never-married black fathers. Also, as shown, black fathers also have a higher likelihood of experiencing widowhood or being separated from legal

Table 1.D. Number (in Thousands) and Percent of Children Living in Father-Only Households by Father's Marital Status, 2006

	Total	Married, spouse absent		Widowed		Divorced		Separated		Married Never	
	#	#	%	#	%	#	%	#	%	#	%
Black	541	26	4.8	28	5.2	137	25.3	63	11.6	287	53
White	2604	167	6.4	101	3.9	1262	48.5	251	9.6	823	31.6

Source: U.S. Census Bureau (2007b, 2007c).

spouses. In this study, the fathers fell fairly close to the national percentages for black single fathers: Half were never married, one-quarter were divorced, and 15 percent were widowed. Unlike the national statistics, none of the respondents here were still legally married and one was an adoptive father.

The degree of involvement in childrearing prior to divorce or separation has also been studied as a possible correlation to subsequent custody. The results have been mixed. Although Gersick (1979) and Greif (1990) found that custodial dads were no more likely to have been involved than other fathers, most studies have indicated a positive correlation between prior involvement and custody (Bartz and Witcher 1978; Hanson 1981, 1986; Risman 1986; Smith and Smith 1981).

Although findings are mixed, researchers tend to conclude that the custodial child's gender plays a role in father custody; fathers are more likely to have custody of boys. For instance, Greif's 1990 study of more than 900 single fathers (96 percent white) found that 42 percent of the fathers had boys only, 27 percent had girls only, and 31 percent had both. Chang and Deinard (1982) found that 57 percent of the households in their study had boys and 43 percent had girls. Meyer and Garasky (1993) found that 56 percent of custodial children in single-father households were boys. A number of researchers (Ihinger-Tallman, Pasley, and Buehler 1995; Marsiglio 1991; Morgan, Lye, and Condran 1988) concluded that the sex of the child may predict involvement on the part of the father because of shared same-sex interests and/or because mothers may press for more father involvement when the child is a son. That gender pattern appears to be the case among black single fathers nationwide as well. According to 2006 Census data, 53.7 percent of children living with fathers only are boys (U.S. Census Bureau 2007b). Unexpectedly, the fathers in this study were more likely to have custody of girls; about 60 percent of the custodial children were daughters. This gender aberration presented a great opportunity to explore how father-daughter custody was experienced differently from father-son custody and is the focus of chapter 5.

In terms of custodial fathers' parenting experience, past studies have found that single fathers tend to assess themselves in a favorable light, but also report loneliness and depression (Katz 1979). Most fathers perceive their relationships with their children as close (Atkins and Rubin 1976; Keshett and Rosenthal 1976; Orthner et al. 1976). Ambert (1982) who conducted a small comparative study of single moms and dads found the fathers to be more satisfied with their parenting than the moms. Hanson (1988) and Orthner et al. (1976) found the majority of dads rated themselves as competent. Even in Greif's 1990 follow-up large-sample survey, which generally found fathers worse off in a number of aspects, such as their social lives, than they had been five years earlier, 80 percent concluded their parenting was "going well." Moreover, when things are going poorly, most single fathers do not seek out a support network (Hanson 1988). Similarly, most single fathers take on the household chores themselves or disburse them among the children; contrary often to the image, they appear no more likely than single moms to seek outside help for household chores.

I offer the above abbreviated summary of research on white fathers only as a point of reference. It is not my intent to transform this study into a comparison between black and white single custodial fathers. Black and white fathers—by virtue of being fathers, male, and American—will have much in common, yet, on average black men face important ecological differences that shape and limit their decisions regarding parenting. Black men, as an aggregate, start with lower educational attainment and incomes and higher unemployment or overrepresentation in the low-wage labor market (which translates into inflexible schedules, part-time employment, and lack of benefits and job security) (Haskins 2006). They more frequently live in neighborhoods with concentrated poverty, more safety concerns, and fewer community resources. This puts them at a "concentrated disadvantage" (Sampson, Raudenbush, and Earls 1997), which is frequently manifested in higher morbidity and mortality. In one study (Anderson, Kohler, and Letiecq 2005) of 127 low-income, mostly African American fathers in urban and rural responsible fatherhood programs, 56 percent, particularly those in rural areas, reported depressive symptoms (nearly four times more than the general population), and 12 percent had health or disability problems. In addition to these social and physical indicators, culturally, black fathers not only face societal doubts about men's ability to parent but also negotiate parenting within a set of stereotypes that paint black men as dangerous and predatory, perpetrators of crime, and likely to abandon their children (Reich 2005). This unequal social and cultural landscape in which black men take up parenting inevitably impacts which men become fathers, how they become parents, and how they perform their paternal role. In turn, black fathers' narratives reflect their vantage point by putting a unique spin on the old yarns of fatherhood.

How This Study Evolved

This study originated when a black single custodial father took my class on race and family. His situation as the primary caregiver of his nine-year-old son stood in contrast to the weight of literature on black fathers. As if finding a gold nugget, I began to scour the city for more like him, hoping he would be the first of many. I relied primarily on word of mouth, working through various local organizations, such as colleges, neighborhood centers, adoption agencies, parenting resource centers, churches, and Islamic centers. I utilized single-father websites (one of the fathers has a personal website in which he details his parenting experience) and the fathers themselves (snowball sampling). Given the relatively small percent of black men in the U.S. population and the even smaller percent of single custodial fathers, recruitment presented a challenge. Over five years I interviewed twenty fathers, most of who resided in Wisconsin's two largest cities. I found two fathers online and two found me after coming across one of my articles. These four fathers resided in Michigan, Arkansas, New York, and New Jersey. Recruitment and interviewing were interrupted twice by hiatuses taken in an attempt to secure grant funding to have the time and money necessary to locate more fathers. However, I was unsuccessful in derailing the current flow of money to studies on nonresident single fathers.

Fathers were sought and admitted to the study based upon their racial identity and custodial status. There was no maximum age limit, but all were over eighteen. "Racial identity" was determined by self-identification. One father was biracial, but he identified more with his African American heritage. "Custodial" was defined as the child residing with the father at least four nights per week, though as it turned out, all of these fathers had custody seven nights a week. Custody could have been formal, that is, legalized through the court, or informal, arranged by the parents or family without the court's intervention. Custody could also have followed a nonmarital birth, divorce, adoption, or widowhood, and all of these precustody statuses were present among this group of fathers.

About fifteen of the fathers had legal custody—that is, custody adjudicated by the courts. Three had been married to the mother and widowed, so they had obtained automatic custody, and two had made informal arrangements with the mother through mutual agreement that father-custody would be more desirable in their individual situations.

Fathers first filled out a quantitative questionnaire that elicited demographic information about themselves and their children and addressed their family background, parenting style and philosophy, existence and proximity of a support system, distribution of household labor and child care, and a limited number of measurable outcomes for child and father. Upon completion of the questionnaire, fathers participated in a two- to four-hour in-depth interview with the primary researcher. Despite the time commitment, all of the fathers agreed to participate in the interview and seemed comfortable doing so.

The interview included questions designed to explore the motivation and factors considered in choosing to parent full-time, definitions of and priority given to various parenting roles, satisfaction with choices made and self-assessment. For example, fathers were asked, "Why did you become a full-time father?" "How did your own childhood family affect your choice to parent?" "What role did your employment (residence, family support, etc.) play in your decision?"

Two of the interviews were conducted via e-mail and one by phone; all of the other interviews were conducted at a mutually agreed-upon time and location, most often the home of the father. Interviews were audiotaped; transcribed verbatim; and then analyzed for common and divergent themes and patterns of behavior, attitude, and experience. All names have been changed to protect their privacy.

What This Study Shows

While I gathered both quantitative, mostly demographic, and qualitative data in this study, the sample is too small to use the quantitative data to determine statistically significant patterns. Because this study was the first in this scholarly niche of fatherhood, I approached it as an exploratory study with no hypotheses proffered. My goal was to produce a richly descriptive study that articulates the choices, identities, and experiences of fathers who take on full-time parenting. I did look at what structural factors—employment, education, housing, for instance—were associated with the fathers' choice to parent, but more importantly I wanted to investigate what meaning fatherhood held for them and how those meanings might motivate their choices about parenting. I sought to examine what roles fathers see themselves playing as parent and how they enact those roles in pragmatic ways with their children in daily life. What sources did they draw upon for constructing their parenting roles? I probed how they construct their identities as fathers, in what ways their identities are constructed for them, and how those identities compete with other identities such as race and gender in ways that might seem antithetical to fatherhood.

To policy makers, these qualitative questions may appear extraneous to their attempts to secure child support and marriage. But if the public concern is really about parenting, these findings have relevance, because identity theory (Fox and Bruce 2001) suggests that men's commitment to children through fathering is a function of (1) the salience of the father role to a man's sense of self, (2) the satisfaction that father role enactment provides, and (3) the perceived assessment of their fathering performance by the fathers themselves as well as significant others. One of the purposes of this book is to illustrate that there are multiple avenues to responsible fatherhood. One does not have to be married to the other parent to be a good parent himself. Although many of these fathers desired marriage or remarriage, one should not have to wait for that to parent well. And although child support is an important and necessary buttress to the sustenance of children, it is an insufficient substitute for caring fathers.

And these *are* caring fathers: as good, loving, and motivated as any other father. Their existence and their experiences deserve public articulation. Though small in number, their stories provide a necessary counterweight to the predominant image of black fathers. Without a doubt I play an interpretive role throughout this book. My race and gender, a white woman, probably influenced the content of the fathers' narratives and my interpretation, but I cannot tell the reader how and to what extent. What I can say is that I have tried to let their voices, their words, paint a picture of this neglected perspective of black fatherhood. And I hope this work will establish a space in the literature for future exploration.

Notes

1. The term *male-headed* is not a synonym for single father. It is possible that some of these male-headed households are older brothers with younger brothers or a grandfather with a grandchild, and so on. But it is an acceptable estimate of single fathers or men who are acting as social fathers of one sort or another.

2. Note also that about 18 percent of black households are married couples with children, which means that fathers are present in those households as well. However, those fathers are not the focus of this book.

༄༅

CHAPTER TWO

Choosing to Parent on Their Own

Lanny's mom was sixteen and his father fifteen when he was born. The young couple divorced when Lanny was in first grade and his younger brother in kindergarten. After Lanny's dad left, Lanny saw him about every two years. Lanny speculates that maybe if he had had a dad around he might have made different decisions, as he himself was eighteen when he had his daughter, Emily, with his girlfriend and twenty when he had a son with another girlfriend. In the military when he found out his girlfriend was pregnant with Emily, Lanny remained in the Reserves and National Guard another eleven years, while he earned a Bachelor's in Education. At the time of the interview, Lanny was a thirty-year-old third-grade teacher in the same school his son attends, and he had had informal custody of Emily about six months. His good college friend Tracy, who is also a single custodial dad, lives in the apartment above him. We sat at his dining room table while he explained that he had custody of his daughter because Emily had been asking to live with him for a couple years. So as soon as he was able to get his own apartment, he let her move in with him. Her mother had married and now had a couple more children. Lanny thinks Emily did not like the new situation at her mother's, and Lanny and Emily's mom are friends, so the mom was amenable to Lanny's taking custody. Lanny continues to pay child support for both children, although he has full custody of his daughter; he fears that if he were to stop, either the mom might get angry and change her mind or the court would intervene and rule that Emily has to return to the mother. He hopes to be able to afford a three-bedroom apartment soon so he can seek custody of his son, although the relationship with his son's mom is not friendly, which might pose an obstacle to custody.

Tracy's parents divorced right before his birth. His mom remarried and had Tracy's younger brother and sister. After the divorce, Tracy saw his dad, who died a few months before our interview, a total of three times after the divorce. Tracy got in trouble in his youth and spent some time in a juvenile detention center. However, he recovered and later attended college. In fact, he was in college when he heard the news that his girlfriend was pregnant. Enthralled with the idea of imminent fatherhood, he returned to his home state and moved in with his girlfriend. Tracy has the clear, winsome voice of a radio announcer, and so he spoke and sang to the baby in the womb. The mother had a difficult pregnancy and labor, so Tracy did much of the caretaking for the baby the first few months. He thinks that contributed to the deep bond he has with his son Train. Eventually he and his girlfriend split; Tracy, energetic and ambitious, said they desired very different lifestyles. Now thirty-one, Tracy works at a social service agency, but I sense he wants more. He seems restrained by his past record and limited opportunities. At the time of our Sunday afternoon interview, his nine-year-old custodial son was with his mom for the day, but his current girlfriend and their newborn son, Tracy Jr., sat in the living room watching television. On the living room wall a photo of Tracy and Train looks across the room to a painting of Malcolm X. During our interview, Lanny comes up to Tracy's apartment to introduce me to his daughter Emily, a polite and bright-eyed girl, who hugs "Uncle" Tracy. Lanny reminds Tracy that he and a couple friends are waiting downstairs for a PlayStation game competition, a signal that we need to draw the interview to a close.

Choice is a highly valued concept in America. Our discourse frequently implies that individual lives are purely manifestations of a multitude of daily—good or bad—personal choices, each building one upon the other, each made in a free market of unlimited options. In regard to family issues, this cultural motif manifests itself in various forms, such as when we are exhorted to choose the "right" mate or when the pro-choice movement advocates reproducing children only at the most advantageous times.

But really the concept of choice is a slippery one. Most social scientists will tell you that all our personal choices are shaped, even constrained, by forces beyond our control—genetic disposition, family income, the neighborhood one lives in, demographic trends, limited cultural imaginations, and laws imposed on us. We don't all have equal options, nor do we select our options from the same menu. We aren't all dealt the same hand, so to speak. Sometimes what appears to be an optimal choice to one appears the lesser of evils to another. She or he may even say, "I had no choice." The truth is somewhere in between.

In regard to the fathers embodied within these pages, some had more choice than others to be biological fathers and, further, to parent. But they *all* had some degree of choice, though they may not have seen it that way themselves; none of them *had* to parent. I make this point because it is often assumed that when black men, especially single men, parent, it is only because they could not escape doing so. In fact, I encountered a paradox in the public's approach to full-time parenting among black men (though I don't claim it would necessarily be exclusive of other men's experience). When black men have conceived children out of wedlock and/or when they are not involved with their children, they are often chastised for making the "wrong" choices. However, when fathers are the residential, primary caregiver, it is frequently assumed that they had no choice, rather than that they had made the "right" choice.

For instance, when I sought a research grant from the National Institutes of Health (NIH) to facilitate this study, a preliminary phone conversation required repeated explanations to make the program officer understand that I was talking about single fathers who co-reside with and parent one or more of their children. The stereotype of the absent black father is so entrenched that the program officer initially assumed that the term *single father* must be referring to single *nonresident* fathers, an unlikely scenario if I had been using the term *single mother*. When the program officer finally understood, he said with surprise, "Oh! Well, there must be something terribly wrong with the mother," the implication being that otherwise these fathers would not be custodial fathers. NIH has been funding the longitudinal study of "fragile families," which focuses on children born to unmarried parents, cohabitants, or single mothers with nonresident fathers. Likewise, the Bush administration has been funding responsible fatherhood programs, which are focused on securing child support from noncustodial fathers, and marriage promotion programs, which encourage low-income fathers to marry the mothers. In this context, the program officer could not conceive of a black father who was parenting by himself, let alone of his own accord.

Later when a colleague of mine at another university began a similar study on single custodial fathers, he submitted his proposal to his university's Institutional Review Board for approval. The board's initial response included criticism for using the word "choose" in relation to fathers who were divorced or widowed, as presumably divorced or widowed fathers were only parenting because they had no choice. Once again, these comments imply that a man doesn't parent unless he has to. As we will see, even divorced and widowed men have other options.

Even scholars who have researched and published extensively on black fathers have frequently overlooked the possibility that black men could be single full-time fathers. Writing in the *American Prospect* (2002) about fatherhood in the black community, Ron Mincy of Columbia University argued that, "unwed parents have four options to choose from: no father-child contact, some father-child contact, cohabitation, and marriage." Father-child custody does not even make his list.

This study's fathers themselves have had similar encounters. While most of the dads said observers give them kudos for taking on full-time parenting (more kudos than single mothers, they assumed), they also noted that such praise walks a fine line between a compliment and an insult. A number of fathers indicated that they received surprised comments such as "She left the children with you?" While the comment suggests there is something unmotherly about the mother—that is, that a good mother would not leave her children—it as well assumes that the father was an unusual choice, perhaps a poor choice, for a guardian. Rubin, whose vignette begins chapter 1, is a divorced father of ten-year-old Kyle. He said that while most people judge him favorably for taking on the responsibility, it's accompanied by the implication that it is only because the mother didn't want to.

> People used to tell me, "how could she just leave her son?" I'd say, "Well, she didn't *leave* her son. I mean, she can see him anytime she wants." He goes over there. And it's not like she just abandoned him on some wayside station. He is with his *dad*. But that's just the society that we live in. I mean people are used to the man taking off.

Such outsider comments, usually from casual acquaintances or coworkers, reflect a perception that fathers are parents of last resort. People often can't conceive that the father may actually be the better parent. Dominic, a father of three children, concurs, "People often assume the mother is a crackhead, but maybe I'm just more interested in being the parent." Darren, too, a divorced father of two preteen daughters, said outsiders admire that he did what so many men don't, but they find it hard to believe that mothers aren't naturally the more devoted parent. He feels he has to convince them that "I sought custody because I knew I was the better parent. I was willing to put aside my desires to raise my children. . . . During the last part of our marriage, I was more willing [than my wife] to stay home with the kids."

I would argue that these fathers in fact have more choice than one would presume. First, biological differences between men and women, combined with the ways American society has constructed gender roles, dictate that men, on average, have more choice than do women in regard to the decision to incur a full-time parenting role once a child is born. Mothers bear the child for nine months; they are the easily identifiable parent; they usually do not require DNA testing to determine their parental status. By social ritual, the child goes home from the hospital with the mother, whether or not she's employed, whether or not she's particularly fond of the infant. In other words, fathering is more sensitive to contextual influences than is mothering (Doherty, Kouneski, and Erickson 1998).

Frequently, fathers can wait until their economic situation improves before they can take custody, as did many of these fathers. The quantitative data indicate that finances and housing were usually in place before fathers took custody. Excluding the adoptive father in this sample, nearly half of the remaining fathers had continuously co-resided with their children since birth; that is, upon termination of the relationship with the mother, the fathers had immediately taken custody. However, the other half of the fathers experienced a period of time when they did not have custody of their child, and some of those fathers were able to use that time to complete a college education, find stable employment, and/or purchase housing, whereupon they requested custody. That time off for personal development and preparation for parenting is an option less frequently available to mothers.

Mothers do have nonparenting options—abortion, adoption, foster care, kin care—available to them, but mothers who take one of these options incur more societal disdain than do fathers, who are virtually expected to seek options other than parenting. Even the widowed fathers in this study, supposedly the ones with the least choice, had options offered to them that mothers aren't often given. (In fact, I did not find these options appearing as frequently in the literature on white single fathers either.) In many cases, family members—in-laws, mothers, sisters, and aunts—offered to rear the children on the father's behalf. Billy, a disabled father of a now college-age son and a teen daughter, said that while he didn't seriously consider relinquishing custody after his wife unexpectedly died, others who knew him in his days of youthful capriciousness expected he might forfeit the children. His in-laws were willing to be involved, but he said they wanted more control than he was willing to concede. Jay, whose vignette begins chapter 1, had not originally wanted children but eventually yielded to his wife's desire for them. When his thirty-eight-year-old wife died unexpectedly, he admitted he thought about giving their three children to family members. "I had several people step up and want my daughter who was ten months old. . . . I had one person step up and want Rory [the oldest son]. Nobody stepped up and wanted Joshua [who had been born premature and had health problems at the time]. So, you know, I sat and I thought about it and I realized 'If I am going to be the caregiver for Joshua, I may as well keep my word [to my wife] and be the caregiver for all three and keep them together.'" Antoine, a young widower and father of a young daughter, said "[A] lot of the in-laws were like 'you should let her stay with Aunty Donna,' and I was like 'why would I want to do that?'"

Sometimes the "offers" come in the form of impositions. Although James had been continuously involved with his daughters before their mother died, his "in-laws" wanted custody of their granddaughters. James recalled,

> They was very unhappy . . . all [the mother's] sisters and brothers, her mother and father. I was in court with them on this issue. When the judge ruled in my favor . . . you know, he said "you can't take these kids away from him." They didn't want me to have the kids, because they said I didn't have a wife and I wasn't able to raise two daughters by myself, but I was determined not to give up and I didn't. I didn't give up, and I didn't miss a day from work and I never missed a court date. Later [the daughters'] grandfather admitted that he was wrong for even taking me to court, and I said, "I have no animosity against you. I hold no grudge. I just want my two daughters to be happy." That's all I want.

Similar to widowhood, maternal incompetence is another factor further muddying the concept of choice. While the definition of incompetence could be debated, three of the mothers would be considered incompetent by most legal standards; two were drug-addicted and one had had several nervous breakdowns. A fourth mother had been living in an overcrowded residence, which led to the baby's injury, so the court placed the infant in foster care. A fifth mother was defined by the father as incompetent because she was unemployed and living with friends. Nevertheless, all the living mothers were in contact with their children, most of them regularly, sometimes spending one or two nights a week together or helping with weekly child care.

Maternal incompetence is often cited as a factor eliminating the father's choice. That is, when a mother is incompetent, it is assumed once again that the father had no choice but to parent. However, options other than father custody, such as formal or informal adoption by other family members, as seen above, do exist. Moreover, state options exist as well. Considering the numbers of African American children who are under state custody, non-father custody is a well-known option that these fathers could have taken. But all the men in this study wanted to avoid that option. Hence, even the fathers in this sample who took custody because their ex-partners were, to one degree or another, incompetent, still view themselves as having freely chosen to parent. Any limitations on their choice, such as a sense of duty or responsibility, were self-imposed.

James, discussed above, was not married to the mother, but their daughters visited him regularly. When the mother died, not only did the mother's parents seek custody, but because he had not been married to the mother, he knew the state could intervene. He said,

> I immediately grabbed [the girls] because I did not want them in the system. . . . I do not want my two daughters in foster care, because I look at the foster care system. You have the people . . . they take these kids in foster care. It's a business; there's no love there. "I want this check for you and you, ok?" You get a monthly check that's just like an income for this custodial person, the foster parents. And I see this happen so much in the system, . . . I think [the] county does have a bad foster care system. I didn't want them in the system, period.

It took James about six months to obtain legal custody because although he had established paternity, he had not had joint legal custody with the mother. He had to obtain the help of a local fatherhood program to achieve custody.

Angelo's infant son had been placed in foster care due to an injury the baby received in the mother's home. Although it was not clear how the baby had been injured, the court decided the overcrowded apartment was not in the best interests of the child. Angelo went to court to prove paternity and took parenting classes in order to gain custody of his son. While he did that, his son was in foster care for about three months.

Kenneth, the custodial father of one young daughter, had suspected that the girl's mother was neglecting the daughter, so he contacted an attorney but discovered it would be quite expensive to hire detectives to investigate the situation. Shortly thereafter, however, he got a call that his daughter had been placed in foster care; the mother had failed a drug test. But Kenneth said that having "custody was always something that was in my mind, you know. I just always felt like I could do it, you know, even before I knew about the drugs. . . . I always felt like I could do a better job of raising my daughter. I mean that was the principal thing." In less than two weeks, Kenneth had his daughter out of foster care.

To recognize that fathers have these options, undesirable as they may be, acknowledges the fathers' agency and infuses their decision to parent with more value. They chose to parent when they could have chosen not to. Nevertheless, for most of the fathers there were practical resources available that facilitated those choices.

Availability of Resources—Employment, Housing, Family, Maturity

In the choice to parent, the availability of resources is often a major, though not always a conscious, consideration. The demographic information gathered for each respondent in this study indicates, for instance, that full-time employment was present at the time of custody in all but one case. By the time of the interview, all but three fathers were still employed full-time; the three were older fathers who were now either retired or disabled and working part-time. About half of the fathers were currently employed more than full-time; that is, several took on part-time jobs as a deejay, an attendant for the disabled, building maintenance, and so on. Only two were receiving some government subsidies in the form of food stamps, housing subsidies, or disability payments. This is congruent with the results of most studies on single fathers, which usually find that single full-time fathers tend to have higher income and more full-time employment and are less likely to rely on (or have access to) various forms of social welfare than single mothers (Chang and Deinard 1982; Dowd 1997; Downey 1994; Gersick 1979; Greif 1985, 1990; Hanson 1985, 1988; Orthner, Brown, and Ferguson 1976; Osgood and Schroeder n.d.; Risman 1986; Santrock and Warshak 1979).

However, this relatively better socioeconomic status is incongruent with the higher levels of unemployment among black men generally. And the higher level of unemployment among black men generally has been debated as a factor determining their lower marriage rates and higher nonmarital birth rates (Mare and Winship 1991; Tucker 1995). Reflecting the complexity of marriage and childbearing decisions, which are usually made by two people at multiple points along a relationship timeline, there is a lack of consensus on the exact role employment plays. For instance, sociologist William J. Wilson (1987) has argued that black men's marriage rates are low due to high unemployment, since both the men and the women view the men as unable to perform the provider role. Testa et al. (1989) also reported that employed inner-city fathers were twice as likely as unemployed fathers to marry the mothers of their children. Moreover, black women's higher levels of education (relative to black men) exacerbates the perception of black men's "marriageability" because women traditionally marry above themselves in education, income, age and so on. However, Lichter et al. (1992) contended that marriageability accounts for some but not all of the race difference in first marriage rates, and Lerman (1993) found that employment didn't make black men more likely to marry, rather it made them less likely to become fathers prior to marriage. In a study of the rise of nonmarital births since the

1960s, Zavodny (1999) concluded that men's employment influences the likelihood that white men will marry their partners following a nonmarital pregnancy but not whether black fathers marry.

Since half of the fathers in this sample were never married, it is likely that employment made them more likely to take on full-time parenting, rather than marriage, once they became fathers (see also Stier and Tienda 1993). Nevertheless, most of the fathers cited employment as a factor they considered but not a driving force in their decision. In fact, several believed that they would have taken custody anyway, even if they had not been employed.

Most of the fathers also had a residence in place when they took custody, and by the time of the interviews, about eight of the twenty fathers owned their residence. Although three fathers had temporarily lived with friends until they could find a place for themselves and their children, most waited until they had secured an appropriate residence before seeking custody. Residence played more of a conscious role for fathers of daughters, probably due to the fathers' perception that they would need separate sleeping quarters for a daughter, while if need be they could share a room with their son. Redmond, for instance, was living with some friends when he took custody of his son, but he waited until he got his grandmother's home to take custody of his younger daughter. Lanny, whose vignette begins this chapter, waited until he was settled in a two-bedroom apartment to get custody of his daughter, Emily, and at the time of the interview he was hoping to be able to move to a larger apartment or house to be able to take his son as well.

Two of the fathers mentioned the mother's overcrowded or dependent living situation as a factor motivating them to seek custody. For instance, John said his recent home ownership was a pivotal reason for taking custody of his young daughter:

> As soon as I bought my home, I wanted my child [Tonya] here with me. Tonya's mother was still living with her mom or her [grand]father, like off and on staying with either one of them, and I just wanted my child to have a home. I mean, when I was younger, I stayed with my grandparents, you know, my mother didn't get a home, didn't even move out of [her parent's] house until I was twelve years old. And I just wanted my daughter to have a place that she can call her own.

Kenneth's former partner had had custody of their daughter, Sara, and they lived in an apartment. Kenneth intentionally bought a house to give Sara "a normal childhood." Note that for these latter men, a home represents part of an idealized vision of how a family, particularly one with children, should be. "A place that she can call her own" is something John hadn't experienced as a child, and for Kenneth, a home is a constituent part of a "normal childhood." Being able to offer this ideal to their children is what many of these men would like to be able to do. Nonetheless, the lack of that ideal didn't prevent fathers from pursuing custody.

In fact, the availability of a human support system, particularly in the form of emotional support, encouragement, and advice, was more prevalent in the fathers' discourse than was employment or housing. Only one of the fathers, the gay adoptive father, said his parents were opposed to his taking custody of a child, but, as often happens with skeptical grandparents, they became supportive once the adoption occurred. Several fathers stated that family members proactively encouraged them to take custody. For instance, John, a twenty-three-year-old plumber and father of three-year-old Tonya, said,

> Well, I knew my family would back me wholeheartedly. When it was first announced that I was having a child, they thought I was young and not ready. But once my baby was born and they seen the responsibility that I was taking for her, they didn't mind at all. They just backed me, helped me out as much as they could. And they were proud that I decided to take custody.

Though most of the fathers resided near family, often within a five-mile radius, none of them lived with family members at the time of the interview (except two fathers who had each taken in a younger brother). It is often assumed that African American single parents are living in extended families, but those findings hold true more for black single moms than single dads (McLanahan and Casper 1995; Meyer and Garasky 1993). Nor did most of these fathers rely on their family members for substantial child care or household assistance. A few fathers, especially older fathers, lived in cities apart from their families or had few living relatives to call upon; other fathers consciously avoided asking family for help because they felt their families had enough burdens to deal with. Most, however, received *occasional* help in the form of laundry, meals, repairs, or financial handouts from various family members or from the child's mom.

The exceptions were the youngest fathers and fathers with the youngest children; two or three of them were receiving assistance in the form of about forty hours of child care per week from family members. One father and daughter lived in the same duplex as his sister and ate most of their meals in her home. Fathers' mothers and sisters are the most common family member assisters, but aunts, grandmothers, brothers, and uncles play an occasional role as well. About one-quarter of the fathers also had girlfriends who helped out, though only Cameron, whose vignette begins chapter 4, was currently cohabiting with a girlfriend.

As mentioned in chapter 1, although findings are mixed, most studies of white single fathers (Greif 1985; Hanson 1986, 1988; Smith and Smith 1981, for instance) indicate that the fathers take on most of the household chores themselves, and children are second in use. Few hire outside the family or use relatives to do household chores. That general pattern is true here as well; most of the men in this study do the majority of the housework themselves, though during one of the interviews, Redmond's teen son vacuumed under my feet in preparation for company they were going to have later that night.

Finally, maturity, measured by age, is also a resource facilitating custody. While the age range of these custodial fathers is quite wide (twenty to seventy-six years old), what they had in common was that the vast majority of them were legal adults when they first became parents. All but one of these fathers were eighteen or older upon the birth of their first child (mothers, on the other hand, were more frequently teen mothers). One-fifth was above thirty when their first child was born. However, most of those who had had children at young ages (twenty or younger) had not taken custody of their children then. Most of those fathers took custody of children they had later in life. For instance, Redmond, the one father who had his first child at the age of sixteen, did not have custody of his first three children. Instead, he has custody of his two youngest children, who were both born when he was in his late twenties and early thirties.

Research on teen fathers indicates that the majority are minimally involved with their children, let alone take full custody, and at least one study suggests that men who first become fathers in their late twenties and early thirties are more involved in child care than younger first-time dads (Hawkins, Christiansen, Sargent, and Hill 1993). Again, it is impossible to know from this sample whether age at birth itself is a determining factor in child custody or whether age, through its correlation to employment and marital status, renders fathers more likely to take custody. A larger sample would be needed to disarticulate the statistical effect of these variables. However, except in the case of Raymond, who felt his "biological clock" was running out, age or maturity did not play a *motivating* role in the qualitative data, that is, the fathers' narratives.

Nevertheless, a couple of the older fathers recognized that maturity played a role in their ability to handle parenting better. Conrad said he wasn't particularly prepared for single parenting; his wife had handled most of the chores and daily child care before their divorce, but he says,

> When it came, I surprised myself, I just fell right into it. I think that maturity had a lot to do with it too. When all of this happened I was at a certain age in my life. I was much better prepared to deal with these things than if I was, let's say, twenty years younger. . . . I was much [more] able or equipped to deal with this sudden change and these responsibilities.

Although based on this limited quantitative data I would argue that absent these resources (employment, residence, social support, maturity) fewer of these fathers would have sought custody, the qualitative data, the fathers' narratives, indicated that these practical resources were not salient considerations in their decisions to take custody. Even without these resources in place, according to most of them, they would have sought custody anyway or at least would have desired to. Recurring throughout their narratives were several motifs of motivation that they say spurred their choice to take on the challenge of full-time parenting: satisfying their own sense of duty and responsibility, fulfilling a special bond with the child, and attempting to break a cycle of distant fathering.

Duty and Responsibility

Studies indicate that women are more likely than men to perceive parenting as a duty, while men view it more as an option (Dowd 1997). However, several fathers here used language indicating that they viewed parenting as a duty. According to them, self-imposed standards, rather than circumstances, compelled their choice, urging them to take on the responsibility. For most of the fathers, the existence and awareness of the above-mentioned noncustodial options constituted the freedom that created the possibility for choice, but their own inner sense of responsibility and accountability rendered those options unattractive.

Tracy, whose vignette begins this chapter, finished college while the mother had custody of Train (a nickname) for several years. He says, if something had happened to the mother,

> I would have had to take him, no matter what my situation. You know what I mean? I would not give that responsibility to nobody. And I wouldn't want nobody else raising my child . . . because I don't want to blame nobody else for how my child turns out. I just want to do the best job I can as a parent, and if my child turns out good, then that's going to make me that much more proud of myself and my child.

While his statement at first indicates that incompetence or death on the part of the mother would have constrained his choice (i.e., he would have *had* to do it), clearly his follow-up statement indicates that the constraint would have emerged from his own desire that he, not anyone else, take the blame or the credit for his child's outcomes.

Likewise, Rubin realizes that his choice to parent as a single father could garner him more kudos than is usual for single mothers. Yet, he says, "People compliment me for having custody, but I don't really warm to the compliments too much, because they are complimenting me on something that I felt was my responsibility to do." Widowed Antoine similarly says of his decision to maintain sole custody of his daughter,

> I was like . . . she's my responsibility. She's my child and I want to take care of her. So that's all I was thinking. So never in my mind did I have like a doubt or think "well, I don't know if I can do this by myself." It's like, just do what you can. I always say, "well God wouldn't give me more than I can handle." I wouldn't want to not be in my child's life. That's just me.

For these men impelled by duty, a sense of responsibility, the choice to rear the child was not a decision separate from the one to create the child; rather, the latter implies the former. Calvin, a never-married father of one preteen daughter, said he felt that "at the end of the day, probably even when she gets older, I'm responsible because I brought her here. So ultimately, as her father, I'm responsible for making sure that she's taken care of properly and adequately." Similarly, Angelo, the thirty-three-old father who went to court to get his infant son out of foster care, indicates that the moral duty to care is embedded in the role of parent, apparently regardless of gender. He says, "I feel I'm doing it because that's what I'm supposed to do. Parents [not mothers or fathers] are supposed to take care of their children. . . . It was my duty to take my son. I feel I'm doing the right thing."

In some cases, underlying their responses was a tone of resentment toward my question regarding *why* they chose to parent. Would I be asking a mother that? Would I be asking a married dad that question? It was as if they were saying, "It's self-evident; I'm the parent, so it's my responsibility." Nevertheless, a couple of the fathers were parenting children who were not biologically theirs—that is, whom they have no legal duty to support—and still others had custody of one or some of their children but not all of them, indicating the presence of other motivations as well.

Fulfilling a Special Dream or Bond

For some of the fathers, taking custody just seemed the natural thing to do, given a long-held desire to be a father, to enact an image they had held of the perfect family, and/or to fulfill the close relationship they had with particular children. These desires to enact the family they had dreamed of and to fulfill the special bond they had with one of their children were difficult to separate, as about half of those who said they had always wanted a family were also those who had developed a special bond with a child. Moreover, most of the time those who indicated the existence of a special bond between father and child were also those who had *one* child and most of the time that child was a boy.

Fathers who were fulfilling a special dream or bond also were more likely to have exhibited a higher level of involvement with the child prior to custody. Either these fathers had co-resided with the mother and child and had performed primary care responsibilities or, during a period of noncustody, they had visited the child frequently and regularly. Nevertheless, taking on a majority of child care responsibilities prior to custody remained the experience of only a minority of the fathers; most indicated that the mothers had handled the majority of the responsibilities previously.

Tracy explains that although the pregnancy with his first son was unplanned, he viewed it as his chance to fulfill his long-held desire to once again be part of an extended family.

> I remember when I was young, very young, all I can remember is my family. Not just my immediate family, but, you know, family all around. So that's what I liked, when I see all the family members together. That's what made me want to establish a family. . . . Although the pregnancy wasn't planned, when I found out my girlfriend was pregnant, I was happy. I was happy. It was a joy to me. It never once crossed my mind that it was a mistake. I didn't try to talk her into getting an abortion or anything like that. It never once crossed my mind.

That desire may have made him more likely to proactively connect with his son, which he attempted to do even as the child was in the womb. Tracy's former girlfriend and the mother of Train is diabetic. Therefore, in addition to his own desire, her ill health during and after the pregnancy required that someone take on more child care responsibilities. Tracy decided that someone would be him.

> I was in Texas in college when I found out she was pregnant. So I dropped out of school. She was very ill through the whole pregnancy, and she had a hard

time in labor. She was in labor maybe thirty hours, and she had to have a C-section to get him out. I stayed up the whole time, till the last hour. I fell asleep in the chair. She was ill after the birth too. I did most of the bathing, diapers, feeding. That was rough, but then I had a new respect for women. Boy I'll tell you that! But before he was born I used to talk to her stomach all the time. I used to sing to her stomach all the time, you know. When he came out I sang that same song, and he knew exactly who it was.

Tracy is a friend and neighbor of Lanny, the custodial father of Emily. Both of these fathers graduated from the same university during a period of non-custody. Tracy's son and Lanny's daughter are close in age, and each of them refer to the other's father as "uncle." Tracy said that even during the period of nonresidence with his son, both he and Lanny tried to see their children as frequently as they could.

When I was at [the University, in a town located about an hour or so from his hometown], I used to come home every weekend and pick him up. I'd take him around the campus and everything, you know, and let him know what college was all about. People there knew him very well. Lanny did the same thing with his daughter. Emily and Train actually grew up together maybe from two years old. When we had free time, we'd say "Let's go get the kids." Every time they [the children] had a break from school, they were with us. We had a lot of people there helping us too. They were surprised that we actually had kids, and they were really surprised that we actually were *into* our kids, were interested in our kids, and into their lives.

Like Tracy, Lanny also said he had always had the "ideal dream as a kid" to "get married the right way, but that didn't happen." However, Lanny says that those years of working on the relationship with his children effected a bond that motivated him to take custody. In particular, his firstborn child, a daughter, consistently expressed a desire to live with Lanny instead of her mother.

We built a bond just a long time ago when she was a baby. Even when I was up at school going two or three months without seeing her, I still could tell. She would run to my arms. And when it was time for me to go, she wasn't ready for me to leave. I mean, she wanted to stay with me. She would really cry, and I would feel so bad. I feel good about it now.

Likewise, a higher level of involvement also preceded Rubin's bond with his child. Rubin was married to his son's mother, and shortly after the birth of Kyle, Rubin's wife returned to work. At that time, she worked second shift at a food store. He describes how they handled child care responsibilities.

When I'd get off work, we'd have an overlap time for both of us maybe of about forty-five minutes. And then she'd go off to work. And she didn't get off until 11 PM, and she had stopped breastfeeding him. So then I was the one who was feeding him. I had to change the diapers and stuff. As I look back on it, I think that was how he and I bonded.

Although Rubin acknowledges some logistical reasons for taking custody—his former wife is now a police officer who works third shift—he says that the real reason is that "[Kyle] and I are kindred spirits. We are the same."

Even though Raymond, the adoptive father whose vignette prefaces chapter 1, did not have the opportunity to establish a bond prior to custody, he said that parenting had been something he had always wanted to do. As did many of the fathers, he drew upon American cultural ideals of a conventional family to build this special dream—white picket fence, the suburbs, a home of one's own, raising children. So after breaking up with a partner, Raymond decided to adopt on his own, at least to fulfill the most important aspects of the dream. After reading Tommy's file and seeing his photo, Raymond was convinced that this was the kid for him. He describes how Tommy helped him fulfill that dream.

I had been wanting to be a father for years. And I always thought about getting into a relationship, have a good relationship, then we can adopt children and have this nice little suburban family with a white picket fence [he says with a chuckle]. Just build a nice little world here, you know. But then I ended my relationship in April of 1995, and I started thinking, "It's going to have to wait again." And then I started thinking, "Why?" Financially, I felt ready. Emotionally, I felt ready. And so I started trying to get information about it. I just felt I could do it. . . . So when his bio was brought to me in June—at the time he was a three-year-old—I took a week to read the file because I didn't want to just make a jump, a quick decision. So I read his file, and when I saw his picture, I just really wanted this kid. . . . The first night, of course, I was infatuated. I just had this little kid, and they left him with me, with *me*.

This desire to enact some form of an idealized family is expressed only among the never-married fathers. Divorced or widowed fathers, having already experienced their own family of procreation, do not articulate that as part of their decision to take custody. In fact, several of the divorced fathers and a couple of the never-married fathers who had cohabited with the mothers of their children concede that they now know establishing a family, particularly an ideal version of one, is not easy, if even possible.

Breaking a Cycle by Turning Absence into Presence

Not unrelated to their desire to fulfill the dream of an idealized family was the striking role played by the fathers' experiences in their families of orientation. Only five of the fathers had grown up in two-parent families. Rather, the majority had spent at least a portion, most at least eleven years, of their childhood in a single-mother family. While this is consistent with the trend of single-parent households being the predominant family structure among black families with children since the late 1980s and seems to support earlier research that finds a pattern of intergenerational single parenting, it doesn't tell the whole story.

The view that these fathers held of their fathers differed significantly from that which they held of their mothers. Three-quarters of them reported being closer to their mother than their father, even though all of the mothers had been employed. Most of the fathers described their mother as a loving, strong, hard-working woman who served as their role model now. At worst, mothers were described as having done the best they could, given a stressful situation. About one-fifth of the fathers found their own father to be nurturing, and sometimes that was qualified by "somewhat." At least half of the fathers had interacted with their own father at best sporadically during their youth. Several could remember seeing their father no more than two or three times. Eight of the fathers said that both of their parents served as role models, although sometimes in the case of the father, it was as a negative role model.

For instance, John, who has custody of three-year-old Tonya, suggests that the positive effect of his father's absence was that it enabled him to know what *not* to do as a parent.

> My mother took care of me most of the time. My father was not there much, though I guess he was there as much as he could. But when someone isn't there, you know, you can't bond with them. A lot of people take their father not being there when they were young as a bad thing. But I just took the good out of it and took what he did do and took what I'm not going to do like him. It definitely made me a better father. It made me say, "I'm not going to do this to my child."

Socialization theories, which often emphasize imitation and modeling as the mechanisms by which children learn, would predict that John and other men who grew up without fathers will fail to learn how to parent. That is, these men would be less likely to take on a parenting role and more likely to reproduce the scenario they grew up in, hence remaining uninvolved and distant should they have children (Gersick 1979; Hanson 1985).

However, rather than reproducing that paternal pattern in their generation, as such theories might suggest, many of these men instead were determined to be the father they hadn't had. Their pain of abandonment gave birth to a narrative of negation; that is, the men expressed strong desires to *not* be like their dads, to *not* produce children who feel toward them the way they felt toward their own fathers. The narrative of Lanny, a third-grade teacher in his city's public school system and father of a daughter and son, illustrates this drive.

> I saw my dad very irregularly. It wasn't even once a year. We might go two years without even hearing from him, and then one day we would hear from him. I remember one time he came and picked up me and my brother and took us to Oscar's [a restaurant], which had a fish tank. It was my first time seeing it. But he didn't even come to my high school graduation, but his brother did. His brother would try to see us once in awhile. The day my baby was born, I said, "I gotta find a better life." I had always said that I was not going to be like my daddy. I mean, I had the idea, the dream, as a kid because of some of the things my mother went through. I said "I don't want my kids to go through any of this shit." . . . But I just said I was *not* going to abandon my kids. We both [he and his girlfriend] could have separate lives, but I was *not* going to abandon my child, no matter what. I think that gave me the drive. . . . I just wanted to raise my kids. You know what I mean? I just wanted—because I never had the opportunity to be with my dad. I just did *not* want to be like my father. [emphasis mine]

Concurring, Lanny's friend Tracy described his similar experience with his unreliable dad.

> I didn't see my dad much. . . . I seen him once when I was four or five. I remember it exactly. I was in kindergarten. Then I didn't see him again until I was in the sixth grade, so I had to be about twelve or eleven. And then I didn't see him again until I was nineteen. So I saw him three times. Then he just passed away this February. And he called once in a while and I'd talk to him. My sisters seen him more than I did, though. Because I didn't really care for him too much, my mother said. Also because I had gotten in some trouble when I was a kid. I was in [a reform school] and I was sent to Wales. And when I got sent to Wales, he sent for my sisters and took them to California, where he lived. He wasn't in the state, you know. That's probably the major reason why I didn't see him. But even when he was here, you know, I don't know . . . why he didn't come see us kids or nothing like that, I can't really say.

Lanny's and Tracy's interactions with their fathers are so few that they can remember the exact details or age at each meeting. Tracy, in particular, appears at a loss to explain (or fearful of the explanation) why his father was so unavailable, particularly to him and particularly at a time when he was in trouble. Hence, as social learning theory would suggest, Tracy acknowledges that the lack of a father left him without a good model to imitate, left him without the knowledge of how to be a good father. But it didn't leave him without the motivation to be different, to be present as a parent. "Being there" for the child becomes the minimum expectation, the least that a father can do. Tracy continues:

So [when my girlfriend became pregnant] I was excited about the baby and her being pregnant. But I wasn't prepared. I mean I didn't know how to be a father. I didn't know anything about that. I mean, my father wasn't around. All I knew is that I was going to be there for him [the baby]. I knew I was going to be there. It was like, you know, I'm not going to do what my father did to me.

While avoiding the reproduction of a negative experience was uppermost in their minds, most of the fathers expressed the desire to create something positive both for themselves and their children from this negative experience. For instance, Theo, the youngest father, with custody of his two-year-old daughter (his vignette prefaces chapter 7), stated:

My real father wasn't there and I always swore to myself that I'm going to have kids that I take care of, which I'm doing. Just trying to offer her more than what I had coming up and being a supportive parent, being there, talking to her. So I'd say the negatives that happened to me growing up ended up turning my life to having me make positive choices about raising my daughter.

Similarly, Rubin had seen his father face-to-face only two times in his life. Like Tracy and Lanny, he could remember the exact settings of those rare occasions. The last time Rubin saw his dad was at his father's funeral. His dad died around the age of forty and his funeral was attended by four people, none of them from Rubin's immediate family. The picture provided a poignant lesson for Rubin, who noted that now at forty-three, he had already outlived his dad. He reflected on his dad:

I saw him twice in life. Once he was doing a mural . . . on the wall of my cousin's basement. And I came over and my cousin said, "there's somebody downstairs that you might want to meet." That's how my family always is, just so deadpan about something like this. So I go down and it was him. And there really wasn't much I said to him. Wasn't much he said to me. The second time

I saw him was in the summer of '74, right after my mom passed. He wasn't at
the funeral, or nothing like that, you know. It didn't really surprise me because
he was never around. . . . Then the next time I saw him was at *his* funeral.
. . . There was only myself, my [two uncles], and the guy waiting to cover up
the grave. My sisters didn't go. It was a very sad funeral. . . . Even at that age
I started realizing that we are all going to make our own decisions and we live
with them.

Rubin took custody of his son immediately after his divorce. He says of that
decision, "I was looking forward to the arrangement because I saw it as a
challenge. And I saw it as an opportunity to do what my father hadn't done."

While this drive to be the kind of father they hadn't had was more prevalent among the men from single-parent families, even some from two-parent
families had similar refrains. Raymond, the gay thirty-two-year-old man who
had adopted six-year-old Tommy, came from a two-parent family. His father
was a church minister.

When I was growing up I played Little League baseball for three years. My father never attended one game. I'm sorry, in three years you can get away for
one game, at least. You know? And he never did. I asked him to go out and
practice with me so I could hit the ball. He bought me a Johnny Batter-Upper
so that I could practice by myself. And, you know, it was like that; if he was going to the store—hardware store, or anything like that and I might have
wanted to go with him, he said, "No, you stay here." It was always like that.
. . . So I had been wanting to be a good father for years.

Antoine, a widower with custody of his daughter, spent most of his life in a
two-parent family; he was nevertheless distant from his father.

I think I wanted to break the cycle, so for all of the things I didn't have as a
kid growing up, I wanted to make sure my daughter has all of that. And . . .
not always materialistic things. . . . The relationship I had with my dad I
wanted to make sure that I had a different relationship with my daughter. So I
guess a better relationship. . . . So it was one of those things that I was like if
or when, you know, I have a child I'm going to break the cycle to do things differently than were I guess presented to me by my father, so I guess I'm not going to go that route or run away or not be there for my child. I am going to be
there and I'm going to do everything I possibly can to make sure that she has
everything that she needs. And, umm I guess, do the best that I can while I am
here. I always know that nothing is guaranteed, so if you want something you
have to go after it. Umm so long as [I am] doing the best [I] possibly can to
make sure that I make a difference.

Although Calvin remembers his dad as a good man, who was "there" for his kids, his father was murdered when Calvin was five. Now as a thirty-something lawyer who fought a long battle for custody of his daughter, Calvin speaks of his choice to rear his daughter after he and his girlfriend split up,

> She's my only child. I was raised in a single parent, I was raised without a father. And very early on I had made a promise, I think even as a boy, that if I ever had a child I will always be there. And ultimately, she's my responsibility. Whether she's with her mother or whomever, she's my responsibility. So, I wanted her with me particularly when I realized that her mother was not going to allow me to be in her life the way I wanted to be. . . . My father was taken from me and my sister. And there was no way that I was not going to be in my daughter's life. So that, it was just pure emotion I think, that commitment and the promise that I had made to myself that was driving everything.

Though we cannot rule it out, one should not conclude from this that the majority of today's adult black men had fathers who were physically or emotionally unavailable. Several studies of fatherhood among two-parent black families indicate relatively high levels of proactive fathering. For instance, Allen's 1981 study of a group of black two-parent families found the fathers to be very involved, and McAdoo's 1981 study of forty black middle-class families found two-thirds of the dads to be nurturing. Also, single custodial fathers represent a minority of men and are not typical of the general population of fathers.

More likely what this indicates is that for the men who do have weak or absent fathers, the experience has the potential to act not as a model to imitate, but rather as a force motivating them to take on more parental responsibilities than is typical of most men. This is not to say that having such experiences will have that effect on the majority of men, but perhaps more than we might expect.

Several recent studies (Baruch and Barnett 1986; Kotre 1984; Snarey 1993) of single fathers, mostly white single fathers, found similar results. John Snarey's 1993 study of single fathers found that fathers whose own father had been a negative role model were more likely than fathers who had had positive role models to *desire* to exhibit more involved fathering. Men who had had positive role models were as likely to go either way in their own parenting. As Snarey (1993), a professor of human development and ethics, explained, rather than modeling what they had experienced and observed growing up, fathers with weak fathers were strongly motivated to "rework their heritage."

Narrative psychologist John Kotre (1984) explains his similar finding by utilizing psychologist Eric Erickson's theory of generativity. In a number of his writings, Erickson (1963, 1964, 1974) argued that humans had an instinct or urge to care for others, which would be manifested at different stages of life through reproduction, parenting, teaching others, and/or in cultural creativity. While it is easiest or most convenient to express this generativity with one's own biological children, it is worth noting here that several of these fathers were also caring for other children in some capacity as well. One father had custody of and was rearing his ex-wife's daughter. Another father was helping to care for, though without custody, the daughter of a former girlfriend (the child was not his biological child). In addition, as mentioned earlier, two of the fathers had younger brothers also residing with them. Three of the fathers had one or more noncustodial biological children whom they saw regularly. Another father had his son's friend living with them as well, and two fathers spent a significant part of their time mentoring other young children through community or school programs.

Conclusion

The quantitative data indicate that practical resources, such as employment, residence, age, and family support, were in place for nearly all of the fathers before they took custody. Fathers weighed such factors in their decision, but these resources did not play a pivotal role in the fathers' discourse about why they took custody. That is, fathers did not appear *motivated* by these factors to pursue custody of their children.

According to psychologist Donald Polkinghorne (1988, 145), "motivation for action is closely related to the capacity to retrieve in the present experiences inherited from the past." The narratives here indicate that the fathers' inherited past experiences remain salient in their present, motivating them to choose parenting and continuing to guide their steps as they make their way through the new territory of full-time parenting. Similarly, Kotre (1984) makes the point that one cannot rewrite one's own history, so one is compelled to rewrite it in a new generation. Yet by reworking one's past in a new generation, one is also repairing one's self and writing one's future. These fathers desire to prevent the "visiting of the sins of the father" upon the next generation. By proactively taking custody of their children, by "being there" for them, these fathers can be the intervening agent who halts or even reverses the consequences of a previous generation's shortcomings, consequences both for themselves and for their children. In a sense, taking the proverbial bull by the horns, they can be the ones to change the course of history, even if it's merely their own microhistory.

CHAPTER THREE

Being All Things to Their Children

Parenting Roles and Behavioral Goals

Reared by his grandparents in Alabama, James saw his parents, who lived in other southern states, during the summers. At age thirty, James had his first son with a girlfriend. They broke up and he had a second son with another girlfriend. Then he returned to his first girlfriend and they had a daughter. James never had custody of these older children, though he established paternity, saw them regularly, and paid child support. Then near the age of forty, James met Rhianna and had two daughters with her, six years apart. When Rhianna died of a heart attack, the daughters were at his apartment and he asked them if they wanted to stay with him. They said yes, and James ultimately went through a custody court battle with Rhianna's parents, who believed a single man could not rear two girls alone. At the time of the interview, James worked four jobs—his full-time job as a city bus driver, which pays a good salary, and two seasonal jobs doing income taxes and lawn and sidewalk care. In addition, he is the manager for his apartment building. His daughters help him fulfill those maintenance duties. James's older children have supported him in handling the custody of these two younger children as well.

Kenneth grew up the youngest of five children in a two-parent family. He was married once for about one and a half years and then divorced before having children. Later he had his daughter, Sara, with another woman, who had custody of Sara for nearly nine years. Kenneth saw Sara regularly during these years, but the last couple years Kenneth noticed that Sara's clothes were often dirty; she was missing a lot of school; her grades were poor; she was eating a lot of junk food and gaining weight; and she was not involved in any extracurricular activities. As a postal carrier, with aspirations to write, Kenneth makes a good salary, so he purchased a house and began to check into the process of seeking custody. But then he got a call that social services had made a visit to Sara's home and had removed her from the home and placed her in foster care. Having already established paternity, Kenneth convinced the court to allow him to take Sara home while the court decided permanent custody. At the time of our interview, he had had full, but temporary, custody for eleven months and was anxiously awaiting the court's decision. Despite his stable employment and the positive changes he had brought into his daughter's life, he was fearful that he would still end up losing custody—so fearful that he was still paying child support to the mother so that she could not use that in court to argue against him.

When researchers have turned their eyes to fatherhood and parenting roles, many have found that fathers and mothers both see the provider role as the primary role for fathers (Leite 2007). No surprise there. The father as provider has been the normative expectation since at least the turn of the twentieth century, and remains the case despite the growth in women's labor force participation and the fact that in 2005 nearly a quarter of employed wives earn more than their husbands (U.S. Census Bureau 2007a). Among unmarried African American fathers as well, Bowman and Sanders (1998) found the provider role remained important even when objective and subjective barriers hindered its fulfillment. The provider role is so entrenched that Hofferth (2003) speculated that married fathers who contribute economically may feel they do not need to contribute to parenting or the running of the household in other ways. Plus, the more hours fathers work in order to provide, the less time they have available to enact other roles, even if so inclined. Consequently, although this unidimensional role for husbands and fathers is declining, society still largely fails to prepare fathers for other parental responsibilities and roles, whether it's housecleaning, nurturing, or disciplining.

In this study, although about half of the fathers had performed household chores—usually the so-called male chores—or babysat for younger siblings, nieces, and nephews while growing up in their families of orientation, only a handful had done a substantial amount of household or parenting chores while they were residing with the child's mother. Hence, only one of the fathers said he felt prepared for being a full-time single father. Indeed, a couple of the men were initially overwhelmed by the totality of the requisite changes the child brought to their routines. Kenneth, whose vignette begins this chapter, was one of those fathers. He is a postal carrier who took custody of his nine-year-old daughter. Although he knew how to do the individual tasks of homemaking, such as cooking, cleaning, and grocery shopping, it was the sum total of all those activities on a daily basis that overwhelmed him. He recalls:

> I mean some of the stuff I wasn't very prepared for . . . and I guess there are certain things that you just can't be prepared for. Umm, you know, actually a lot of the stuff was a surprise, like combing her hair and stuff like that. I really don't have a big problem with it, but when she first came over, it took me a lot longer than it probably would take her mom to do her hair in the morning or if I did it in the evening or whatever, but that's the kind of stuff I wasn't familiar with. I have at least one, two, three, nieces that, you know, I helped out with when they were in town or whatever. I actually did some babysitting when I was a teenager. So you know some of those things, you know, there was a learning process but it wasn't a big deal. . . . But when she first came into the home when I was working and I was working long hours, . . . like seven o'clock or later, and I would want to pick her up from the lady who does after-school care. Actually I would take her to the woman's home and then later I would pick her up from her home. You know, if we had grocery shopping or anything and I didn't have any clothes for her, so a lot of nights we would run out and buy one to two outfits for her. So we wouldn't get to the house till eight or so. Cooking dinner, ah you know, sit down eat together, she'd take a bath, I'd do whatever to her hair and everything. I'd have the dishes and have to clean the kitchen, fold laundry and stuff like that. So a lot of time I wouldn't get into bed till like eleven o'clock. Doing the same thing over and over and over, every day for two or three weeks, I was just exhausted. I mean just exhausted. I think about a month in I hit a wall, I found that when I was off from work, I don't know, it was my regular off day or if it was Sunday or what, I just slept all day. I mean slept all day. I just couldn't move, and umm, I think that was a big adjustment, just trying to get the two of us into a routine where we could fit everything that had to be done into a day.

The ones who expressed the strongest feelings of unpreparedness were those who had infants or whose children had behavioral problems. For instance, Angelo, father of one-year-old Angelo Jr., echoed the complaints of many new parents.

> It was kind of a shock when I first started keeping him. He was a month old. And he would not go to sleep. Fifteen or twenty minutes and he was up. He'd sleep at the most half an hour. He'd get up—at night, mainly at night. They get their days and nights mixed up. I'd take his bottle. I'd have to walk him around for half an hour. It was awful. That would go on the whole night. But as he gets older, it's getting better, but he don't sleep through the night yet. I

guess it's just something that they go through. There's no remedy for it. I thought taking care of my nieces and nephews had kind of prepared me for that, but I didn't keep them when they were that young.

Raymond, the father of Tommy, who was a special-needs adoption, recounted their first three weeks together.

The first night, of course, I was infatuated. I just, I had this little kid, and they left him with *me* [he laughs]. And they left him with me. He didn't want to go to bed by himself that night. So I laid on his bed until he fell asleep and then I got up and went back to my room. And then the next day was hell. It was hell for three weeks. But again, he was just being taken from one home and put in another, with no choice about it. Like I said, that first three weeks was just hell. I actually thought, "Why did I do this?" Everybody told me this was going to be hard. And I said, "No, I can't go back and say I can't do this." Everybody would have said, "I told you so." So, you know, it was really those first three weeks. The thing is that I think I was also arrogant about it. I was doing so well in my career, and I was doing well in the community as well. I was on the board of directors for the Gay, Lesbian, and Bisexual Services Center in [a Western state]. So I was a recognized leader in the community. I was a member of the governor's staff. I was a recognized leader in the recycling industry. You know. I think part of it was I was just arrogant. I thought, I can do this. Just bring this child on. I'll make the difference [he laughs]. You know, all you have to do is give them food, and you know, give them love, and help them with homework. And I had no idea that that was 1 percent. . . . One of the things I told Social Services that I've learned in my short period of time of being a parent is that being a parent and making the decisions are all one big guess. And the thing you figured out this week will change next week. And you have to guess again.

Despite their lack of preparation for parenthood, none of the men sought out other single fathers for support or commiseration. (This is somewhat distinct from studies of white single fathers, such as Tedder, Libbee, and Scherman [1981], but particularly Greif's [1985], who located most of his respondents—and had larger sample sizes than most other single-father studies—through single-parent support groups.) Only one of the fathers in this study took a parenting course, and that was court ordered as part of his paternity application. As mentioned in chapter 2, two of the fathers—Lanny and Tracy—are friends, lived in the same apartment building at the time of the interview, and socialize with each other and their children. While they do support each other in parenting, such as giving advice to each other's children, they had been friends since college and did not specifically seek each other out due to their parental status. Many fathers minimized help seeking for several reasons: they preferred autonomy, they didn't want to burden family members, or they hadn't felt a strong need for it. When fathers did seek advice, some looked to grandparents or siblings as role models of good parenting or for advice, but the most frequent source of advice was their own moms. As mentioned in chapter 2, mothers were also most frequently cited as their parenting role models. The characteristics admired in mothers included their teaching of independence, exhibiting optimism or family values, and giving guidance. But the most admired characteristic was their staying power. When things got tough, the fathers reminded themselves that their mom had done this and more as a lone parent. Several fathers echoed Angelo when speaking of their mothers:

> She's a very strong person. I mean, to raise me and my five sisters pretty much on her own, through a lot of tough times. And to make it through the tough times, she needed a lot of strength. She's special. We didn't have a lot growing up, but she made us feel special. We didn't have a lot of material things and stuff like that. But she showed us a lot of love. So if she can do it back then, not making a whole lot of money and raising five of us, I should be able to do it with one.

Ironically, a few of the fathers took advice from their children about how to parent better, and surprisingly, the advice was not always to be more lenient. After Billy's wife died, he tried to deal with his two children with kid gloves to assuage their pain and make up for the loss of their mother.

> [In fact,] Otto . . . made me grow up. He said, "Dad, when you tell us to do something, you should just go ahead and make us do it." And, you know, that is kind of shocking to hear your fifteen-, sixteen-year-old son tell you that. He said, "Dad, you don't follow through on your punishment. When you put us on punishment, leave us on punishment. When you tell us to do something, make us get up and do it right then." I was proud and then again I was mad and shocked at it, but I was proud of the fact that he recognized those things. And was able to tell me those things, not holding them up inside. And I think that's going to make him a better parent.

Similarly, a couple other fathers noted that their children had justifiably highlighted incidents where the fathers had been inconsistent. Jay, for example, said that his oldest son Rory pointed out to him that Jay had always let the middle son quit commitments, such as team sports, while he made Rory finish what he started. The middle son had had health issues as a young child, and looking back, Jay says "Maybe I was soft on him because he was the sick one."

However, several of the men looked to less conventional sources for their parenting ideals or advice. Three fathers cited *The Bill Cosby Show* as a role model for parenting styles (for a summary of the debate over the *Cosby Show*'s depiction of fatherhood, see Chan's 2006 article). Calvin confessed: "I feel a little silly saying this, but Bill Cosby. Really, I mean, I grew up on the Cosby show. And I idealize that show, and I idealize him as a father figure. . . . On TV, Cosby seems to be very involved and loving to his kids." As will become apparent later in the chapter, Raymond attempts to adopt the television Cosby father's "wise old sarcastic attitude in front of the children." Also, a sign of the times, two of the fathers, who were contacted through online websites, look to web sources and online parenting chat rooms on the Internet. For instance, Amar posted a question about whether he should let his fourteen-year-old daughter wear lipstick. Within a short period of time, he had an array of replies, mostly from women, falling within the chasm between yes and no. He uses their feedback to acquire different parenting methods and reasoning, as well as to gauge how realistic his expectations are.

Parenting Identities: Multiple Roles

Like most single parents, single custodial fathers have less opportunity to pick one role and leave the others to someone else. They are usually the sole providers, but unlike married fathers, who theoretically could distribute the workload to their wives so that providing could be their only role, single fathers must be all things to their children. As Jay said, "as a single father, I'm not just the father, I'm the mother. I'm the Santa Claus, the caregiver. I gotta be their best friend. I gotta be everything to these children." Consequently, while many studies present only two roles—nurturer/caretaker or provider (for instance, see Wille [1995] and Lewis [2001])—I offered single fathers multiple identity options, because I not only wanted to investigate how they see themselves but how they *enact* their parenting.

On the questionnaire, fathers were given six possible parenting roles and asked to prioritize them according to their importance (with one being most important and six being least important) in defining their own fathering identity. The six given roles were provider, nurturer, teacher, disciplinarian, authority figure, and friend. Later, in the qualitative interview, the fathers were asked to explain why they ranked the roles as they did and to define what those roles meant to them by illustrating how they enact that role with their children. They were also asked to add any other roles that might be important to them and to discuss what it means to be a "good father."

The Top Two: Provider and Nurturer

As shown in table 3.A, 75 percent of the fathers listed provider as first or second in importance, confirming other studies (McAdoo 1993; Taylor, Leashore, and Toliver 1988) that have found the provider role to be an important part of African American male identity. However, nurturer came in second; 55 percent of the fathers listed nurturer in the first or second place of importance. No other role came close to those. Friend, disciplinarian, and authority figure were ranked in the two least important categories by a majority of the fathers; 60 percent of dads placed friend and disciplinarian in the bottom two positions of importance; 55 percent did so for authority figure.

The men's level of education or income and their family background (i.e., single-parent or two-parent) did not appear to have much impact on which roles they ranked as the two most and least important. However, as mentioned earlier, among the fathers who did not have custody all along, all were employed when they took custody, which probably indicates that their ability to provide was an important, even if subconscious, factor in their initial custody decision.

The ways the fathers define and play these roles might give us some clues to explain these rankings. Although 75 percent of all fathers put provider as first in importance, most of the fathers did not have much to say about being a provider. Most viewed it as a "given." Even those who placed it first in importance tended to view it as a necessary but insufficient factor in their parenting.

The provider role was perceived as the "bare minimum" that *had* to be enacted in order to fully play the other roles. Billy, a father disabled by diabetes and dual hip replacement surgeries, said:

> I had to take care of their needs, 'cause without taking care of their needs, nothing else could fall in place. Because if a kid woke up hungry, there's not too many things you could tell him. If the kid didn't have a place to lay his head, you know, what kind of rules could you instill or what kind of teaching could you do? So, providing for a person the best that you could do has always been number one with me. Then it becomes something that you can put in the back of your mind. Anything that you don't have to give a second thought to is good.

Table 3.A. Rankings of Parental Roles by Number of Fathers

Importance of role	Provider	Nurturer	Friend	Authority Figure	Teacher	Disciplinarian
Ranked 1–2	15	11	1	5	5	3
Ranked 3–4	4	8	7	4	12	5
Ranked 5–6	1	1	12	11	3	12

Nevertheless, a couple men, particularly those who grew up in poverty, thought the provider role was important in and of itself, not merely as a facilitator for other roles (see also Christiansen and Palkovitz 2001 for a recent study reinstating the provider role as pivotal for fathers, though not mothers). For instance, Dominic said, "I think provider's important. I mean, I don't want my kids to go without. I went without a lot of things, just because of the socioeconomic environment I grew up in. And so that's definitely very important to me." Still, he listed that role as second in importance to nurturer, because "you can't supplant all the listening, all the supportive stuff with just items."

A couple of fathers also made a point of distinguishing that their obligation as provider was to provide only for the *needs* of their children, not necessarily their *wants*. For instance, Jay, whose three children are nearly adults, said providing was his number one role, but he defined provision narrowly:

> The number one principle that I wanted them to learn is that I will always provide their needs. I would try to give them their wants, but their wants aren't guaranteed. I'll give them their needs until they turn nineteen. You need food, you need a roof over your head, you need clothes on your back. It may not be what you want, but it will be what you need.

As mentioned before, a number of the fathers worked more than one job; one was working four jobs; one was about to lose his job, so fulfilling the provider role consumed much of their time and physical and mental energy. Nonetheless, the other parenting roles garnered much more attention in their conversations. Fathers found the roles of nurturer, teacher, and friend more interesting and easier to illustrate their enactment.

Fathers defined "nurturer" largely as "being there," particularly in times of disappointment or joy; giving affection; listening; and making sure children know they are loved. This also is congruent with previous studies of black fathers in two-parent families. Most of those studies have found nurturance to be the predominant mode in father-child interactions (Bowman 1993, McAdoo 1981). Moreover, Allen and Doherty's (1998) study of adolescent single, nonresident black fathers found that the fathers defined fathering predominantly and literally in terms of "being there."

Raymond, a state employee and father of Tommy, who became his son after having been in nine foster homes, ranked nurturing first.

> Tommy needed someone who would just love him. You know despite all the hollering, despite all the screaming, the bed-wetting, the bad table manners, just everything he was doing and going through, he needed someone just to

love him. And so that was very important. There were days I wanted to just pull my hair out, you know, but that's the first thing—I needed to make sure he knew that he was safe. He needed to feel safe, and so I did a lot of holding him. Holding him in my lap. And even sometimes for time-outs that he had to take, I would hold him for the time-out. And, you know, he needed that. He needed a lot of that. He needed to know I was going to be there.

Similarly, Calvin, a lobbyist and father of a daughter, defined nurturer as "someone who is there for her. Someone that is her supporter; that is where my focus is. It is . . . more important for me, for her, to know that I'm some-one that . . . that I love her and that I'm there for her and that I will always be there for her.

"Being there" suggests a stability, a commitment, an assurance to the child that the father's presence is abiding and independent of the child's behavior. As pointed out in chapter 2, in many cases, this father constancy had been absent in the fathers' own childhood experiences.

James, whose vignette prefaces this chapter, is an enthusiastic man who had custody of the two youngest of his five children. He defined nurturing more in terms of affection.

> They love to be hugged. Something goes wrong sometimes, and I give the big girl a hug and say "It'll be better" or "Don't worry about it. Daddy will handle it." The little girl, she likes daddy. She likes for me to read to her. She likes me to cuddle her, and sometimes I tease her, "You know what? I'm going to give you away." She says, "No, you're not. You love me." And I say, "Yeah, I love you."

Dominic who has three children, two girls and a boy, defined nurturing as listening:

> Listening to their needs, to their desires. Or just hearing them . . . if you don't listen to people, you don't know what they want, what they need, and you're being ineffective as a parent. I can give you a thousand and one exam-ples. When Marcia [his youngest daughter] said she had, just today, a blister on her foot. I took the time to look at it and see if it needed to be covered or just hearing her complain even though it wasn't really a blister yet. Just hearing her and saying "Ok, we'll do something about that."

Although the definitions vary, most of them have in common the theme that nurturing requires being in the presence of the child in such a way that the child is aware of and *feels* the father's presence through his or her senses—sight, touch, hearing—as well as emotionally.

The Middle Role—Teacher

Teaching was ranked middle to high in importance, and the fathers' discourse tended to indicate that several fathers viewed teaching and nurturing as highly intertwined. Teaching can be accomplished through example or by direct conversation (or in parent lingo, lecturing). Rubin, father of Kyle, was one of five fathers who ranked teaching at the top of their list and who viewed most of his interaction with his child as a teaching moment. Not unexpectedly, Rubin worked in the public school system as a paraprofessional. He explained how he viewed his main parental role.

> Teaching is the end-all be-all of me as a parent. I think being a teacher is important, especially in the situation I'm in, I'm teaching him all things. Not just his academics. But I'm teaching him manners, common sense, how to think things out for himself. Like when we go bike riding through this park that's not too far from here, he gets in front of me, and I'm always saying, "When you ride a bike, never ride a bike blindly. Always look. Look for cars, look for cars coming out, look for people walking out. If you come up to a corner where it's a blind corner, like a building where you can't see what's coming, cover your brakes and slow down, because there could be another bike coming around the corner." You know, that type of stuff.

Most of the fathers viewed teaching in pragmatic terms—teaching daily life skills such as household chores, taking care of one's self, and social manners. Fathers of young children understandably focused on basic daily self-care skills. For instance, in addition to safe bike riding, Rubin also mentioned with some chagrin that his most recent teaching moment was helping Kyle learn how to successfully aim for the toilet, as he was tired of wiping up off-target droplets here and there. Raymond also discusses the daily caretaking skills he needed to teach Tommy, shortly after the adoption.

> Tommy had a lot of things to learn. But I had to recognize that part of teaching is recognizing when this is not something we have to learn right now. And so, you know, at the beginning—a child who is four years old generally knows how to bathe himself. Eating—he was very unaware and to some extent still is of what his body is doing. And so he would have food in his hair, all over his face, down around on the floor, on the table. There were different things he needed to be taught. He didn't know how to tie his shoes. He didn't really know how to button up things. And he still doesn't know how to dress himself nicely. And that's [he says with a laugh] only because I think that's his male heterosexuality coming out.

As mentioned earlier, James works four jobs—bus driver, building manager, income tax preparation, mowing and shoveling business—and he wanted his daughters to know how to do their own chores.

> When they first came to me to live, I had to get up every morning to iron their clothes, or we'd do them at night. We chose the clothes and lay them out and ironed them, whatever. Now I'm saying, "Ok, you're twelve years old, you need to know what you want to wear to school, lay it out, and iron it. You do your homework, you iron your clothes." So now I'm teaching the little girl how to iron her clothes. I taught the big girl how to do laundry; you put the colors here and the whites there, and you set the machine, and put a cup of soap and let it wash. So I taught her all that. It didn't take her long to learn. She's a very bright kid, but it didn't take her long to get lazy too. "Oh, I'm tired." So I don't put all the laundry off on her; we share it.

Many of the children contributed to household maintenance by keeping their rooms clean or taking out the garbage, but most of the fathers did the majority of chores themselves, either because their kids were too young to perform the chores satisfactorily or because they wanted their kids to focus on school or extracurricular activities. Antoine had taught his daughter to make a "pretty mean meatloaf." Jay, who admitted that he himself was messy and didn't put a lot of emphasis on chores, still wanted his sons to see that it was no big deal to do household chores, the same way Jay's mother had taught him that it was "no big deal for a boy to go to the store and buy Kotex." James's and Lanny's families either ate out or ordered in the majority of their meals, as neither they nor their children had sufficient cooking skills.

To his teaching list, James also added interpersonal skills, particularly respect for authority figures and the elderly, as his daily contact with the public through his job as a city bus driver led him to believe these were declining values and manners in America. When asked what he teaches his daughters, he answered,

> How to respect another human being. Don't disrespect your teachers or another adult, you know? Being a bus driver and with the public each day, I see so many young kids out here who disrespect the elder people, and I don't want my kids growing up like that, to disrespect no one. They go to church. They do things by themselves, and they do not disrespect no one. That I will not allow—to disrespect another human being in no kind of way.

Billy also addressed interpersonal skills, such as good manners, for his daughter.

[Saying] yes, no, thank you, excuse me. That's being polite. I have always taught her to speak to everybody, greet everybody. Amelia questioned me, "Well, what if they don't speak back?" Makes no difference, you have spoke to them, move on. I have had so many of her teachers in grade school and junior high come back to me and say "What have you done? Your daughter speaks to everybody." Job done. Lesson taught. I'm happy. [This concern for respecting others will come up again in chapter 5 on racial socialization.]

Nevertheless, the single most frequently mentioned teaching lesson was related to financial skills. Fathers wanted their children to be sophisticated about finances. Antoine, an IT manager, has an eleven-year-old daughter. He was already trying to develop an entrepreneurial mind-set in her.

We talk about bills and even at this stage of the game I teach her about credit cards and the pros and cons of having them. You know, when we're at the Laundromat or something, I teach her about putting things into perspective, like "you have so many machines and if you have so many people using those machines who are putting the dollar in the machines. How much money do you think the business owner is going to make off of the dryers and washing machines?" So I feel like the entrepreneur teacher of some sort.

Kenneth, the postal carrier who is looking for a less time-consuming job, says he wants his nine-year-old daughter to have an early understanding of how to develop financial assets.

I have already, early on, had her opening up a bank account. So I can teach her how money works, how you earn money, how you save it, how you accrue interest, how you can use money to earn more money, because I want her to have understanding of that. I didn't really have understanding of that when I left home. I had to learn that stuff on the fly and everything.

The Roles They Love to Hate—Friend,
Authority Figure, Disciplinarian

At the other end of the importance scale, "friend" ranked low to middle. Fathers often perceived the role of "friend" to be in opposition to parental authority, and most of them did not want too much of either. Only one father, James, said he currently viewed himself as his children's best friend, but that was partly because his daughter was in a phase where she didn't have many friends. And given the amount of time he spent at work, he also did not have much time to socialize. He explains:

Well, you know what? I feel like right now they're my best friends. To me, I'm a dad and their best friend, and to them, they think the same because my daughter, she don't have no friends. At school, just a few. As a teenager, fifteen, you'd think she be into boys and have a lot of friends. No, she's not into that. Sometimes the school worries about why she doesn't have a lot of friends.

But most fathers wanted to have a friendlike relationship with their children only in moderation. Consequently, some fathers discussed how they wanted to be a friend in the sense of hoping that their children would feel comfortable enough to confide in them and talk openly, particularly about sex. For instance, several fathers spoke as Tracy did,

> I think kids kind of get lost, especially at his age [middle school]. And I think they need their parents to be their friend. You know, so he can just feel free, he can come and talk to me about anything. I talk to him about sex. I've been talking to him about sex since he was six years old—you know, about condoms, sex, I mean everything. I laid it all out on the line. I mean, I made sure he gets that, because I don't want him sneaking behind my back trying to be curious about something. That's part of my friendship with him.

Antoine also said he didn't always have to be the authority figure; friend was a role he could sometimes play to his daughter.

> It's like I can also be someone that if something's bothering you or your feelings were hurt or someone said something, you can always tell me about anything. I've tried to respond to things, where I could have gotten angry, in a way that when she gets to be an adult or she gets into the preteens, which they say is supposed to be like the scariest part, that I have done everything to make sure that she [can] talk to me about anything. I'm always there trying to give her my undivided attention.

As illustrated by Tracy and Antoine, many of the fathers' comments associated being a friend with intimate conversation. Calvin also wanted to be able to build the camaraderie and trust that would be required to enable his children to talk openly, but he admitted that talking to his daughter about boys, sex, and menstruation did not come easily to him. (This theme will be discussed in more detail in chapter 4). He confesses:

> As a friend, I try to talk to her about boys and it is very difficult for me. You know, I have to just make her feel like she can talk to me about anything. I tried to talk to her about her period . . . , but that did not go anywhere. But at least she knows that I'm comfortable. Well, I'm not really comfortable, but I get over it because I just want her to know that we can talk about anything.

On the other hand, fathers recognized times when the perceived interests of father and child may diverge, and the fathers might need to call upon their parental authority. Theo, father of preschooler Jacqui, explains:

> We are friends, but not all the time. When I'm trying to teach, discipline, and provide, I'm not always her friend. She'll say to me "You're not my friend anymore." Then I say, "I don't have to be your friend; I'm your dad." But friend means that she trusts me, she tells me things.

Rubin's handling of church attendance also reflects this need to balance the roles of friend and authority. Rubin's sister takes Kyle to church every Sunday, but Rubin, who attended church as a child but is no longer "interested in getting my spirituality from Second and Main [the location of the church]," does not attend with him. Rubin says that other people and Kyle have asked why Kyle should have to go if his father doesn't. He answers:

> I made the decision not to go as an adult, and I tell him "This is how I run things. There's a lot of things you'll be able to do when you become an adult. But at this point there are times when I have to take on the role of parent and decide what's best for you." I used an example, I said, "I don't go to school with you. I don't go to your music lessons with you, but you are getting knowledge from both of these. You are learning something from them. And you don't have to have me sitting there with you."

Finally, a couple fathers felt that being a friend to their children was inappropriate and would have deleterious effects for their children's outcomes. For instance, Billy said that after his wife died, he had tried being a friend to his children, by which he meant he was lenient and bought them a lot of things. He felt that was a failed policy and now took a more authoritarian mode. He explains:

> A year ago I would have put [friend] higher, but I am still learning that I couldn't be a friend to my kids because my kids learned me quicker than I learned them. If I said "No" to my kids, my kids didn't even argue, they outwaited me. They knew I was eventually going to come around. And I did. Eventually I would give in without them saying a word. So, friendship and parenting don't mix.

Like Billy, Kenneth also thought that the friend role was least important. He believes too many parents have gone in that direction with their children. Nonetheless, note that he wants to have the same relationship, where the children feel free to talk and relate to the parent, as do the fathers who think a friend is an acceptable role to play at least occasionally. He also enjoys the idea that his daughter currently thinks of him as a friend.

> A lot of problems that kids have now is that parents are too friendly with their kids. I think you have to do that nurturing thing. You have to have a good relationship with them. They have to be able to talk to you and relate to you and everything, but I don't think that you can necessarily be a good parent if you are really good friends with your child, because a friend is a peer and I don't think that a child is a parent's peer. They need discipline and authority that I just don't think that you can carry off when you're a friend. But if you ask Sara, I would think she would tell you that I am her friend. I do like to make sure we have fun together and everything.

Despite the recognition that at times parents need to assert their authority, "authority figure" was also ranked low on the scale by most fathers. Most fathers viewed an authority figure as having the last word, making the rules, being in charge. Billy said being the authority figure means that "I'm the final word. You can argue as long as I feel like arguing; last word is going to be mine. Period." But many fathers regarded the role of authority figure somewhat negatively. Fathers thought an authority figure role had the possibility of inducing fear, not respect, in their children, and so they thought that that role should be played as a last resort. Several made comments to the same effect as Angelo, father of one-year-old Angelo Jr., who stated, "If you are doing the nurturing and the teaching and providing the discipline as a positive reward, then authority isn't necessary."

Interestingly, the five fathers who ranked authority in first or second place were all older, and two of them have children with some behavioral problems; one of the latter fathers was Raymond, the special-needs adoptive father of Tommy, and the other was Redmond, whose teen-aged daughter was in counseling at the time of the interview. While I can't test the cause-effect direction here, it may be that parents who have children exhibiting behavioral problems feel more need to call upon the authoritarian role, thus indicating that a child's behavior can be just as influential in shaping the parents' roles as vice versa.

Related to the authority figure role was disciplinarian, which was ranked middle to low in importance. As with the other roles, fathers' views of discipline varied, but tended to be defined either as punishment and correction of poor behavior or as cultivating consistency and good habits (closer to the definition of teaching). Nevertheless, the distinction in definition didn't appear to have a significant impact on ranking. In relation to discipline, fathers were asked specifically whether and under what circumstances they used corporal punishment. In order to address these aspects, I want to first elaborate on the behavioral goals or expectations fathers had for their children.

On the questionnaire, fathers were given ten behavioral goals that they were supposed to rank as "very important," "somewhat important," "not so important," or "not at all important." Each goal was stated in a declarative statement: I want my child(ren) to

respect their teachers and other authority figures
obey me
be honest
be creative
be polite and considerate of others
have compassion for others
succeed academically
be independent and self-reliant
have high self-esteem
get along with others

Because fathers were not required to rank each goal relative to the others, the result was that there was little variation among the goals; all of the goals were ranked by all of the fathers as somewhat or very important. Some of the fathers ranked all of the goals as very important. Still, the fathers' narratives tell us something about how they viewed these goals, and clearly they discussed these goals in more nuanced terms than a survey would normally allow.

The goals that were most frequently ranked as only "somewhat important" were creativity, willingness to try new things, and getting along with others. The commonality among those three goals is the fathers' underlying fear that children who might be free-spirited or too willing to try new things or too concerned about getting along with their friends might also be more susceptible to peer pressure, activities that might lead to troublesome behaviors, or to problematic responses from others. For instance, Billy said,

Being creative, being very creative, you are going to find so many obstacles and you are going to get your feelings hurt. You will always be questioned. You can get your ideas shot down relatively easy by people louder than you.

Most fathers who gave examples of things they would like their children to be willing to try listed food, which I will address more in chapter 5, but fathers also expressed limitations on willingness to try new things as well. Antoine said of his daughter, "I try to make sure she's willing to try new foods, to branch out. But you got to know when to lead and when to follow, when to try new things and when not." A willingness to try new things needed to be tempered with an ability to discern among appropriate behaviors.

Interestingly, although fathers ranked obedience and politeness as very important, the fathers desired neither absolute obedience nor polite consideration of others. Underlying the narratives explicating both of those goals was the message that in them there could be too much of a good thing. Similar to their worries about their children's willingness to try new things, fathers thought obedience and politeness could lead to unsafe situations or a lack of self-respect. For instance, Antoine says that for him obedience was mostly a safety issue; that is, he wants his daughter to obey him because he has her safety in mind. However, he noted that his daughter has a "spunky attitude," which he doesn't want to dampen. "I never want to break that. I want her to be able to stand on her own two feet." Similarly, Calvin said, "you know I was somewhat of a rebel, and so I think a little rebellion and questioning of authority can be a good thing." Jay also said,

> I don't want robots. I want them to do what they know is right to do, only because through the process of trial and error they figured it out. Now if that means obeying me because I'm telling them right now at this moment . . . if I should ask Brie to go to the store and get me a loaf of bread, and she says "OK, give me the money," now that's obeying. But the process of trial and error, of letting her make decisions on her own, of failing on her own, I really believe that's the reason she's getting up and going to the store. They're defiant children, and I've raised them to be that way.

The potential hazards of being overly polite were pointed out by a couple of the fathers. Antoine said: "I definitely want her to be polite and considerate of others, but I guess not *too* polite where it would compromise, like, for example, a stranger speaks to you, and [the kid thinks], 'my dad told me to be polite so I should speak.'" And Kenneth, noting that his views are a change from his own parents, who would have required him to say "yes, ma'am, no, ma'am," advocated moderation in courtesy as a way of maintaining self-respect and safety. He elaborates,

> Being polite to others is important but I don't think that is an essential . . . because some people don't deserve for you to be polite to them. I tend to stress to her to treat people as they treat her or treat them as they deserve to be treated. . . . But I don't think that she needs to be polite to everybody because I feel like if I program that into her then that will be something that will make her more susceptible to peer pressure.

Although the quantitative data failed to sort out much variation among the most important goals, the fathers' discourse highlighted the goal of independence and self-reliance as the most desirable. However, their definitions of independence varied slightly. Rubin elaborated on the importance of independence and how he senses that parents are de-emphasizing this goal in today's parenting. Note that this is also very much tied into his parenting role as teacher; for Rubin, teaching life skills, such as laundry, cooking, and budgeting, is about independence. Yet, ultimately, independence is also an attitude, a willingness to take responsibility, to be accountable, for one's own actions.

> I emphasize to [Kyle] that I'm raising him pretty much as a parent in the wild would, in the sense that I'm raising him to be independent. Because I think one problem with a lot of kids—and you see examples of it with some of the young people out here—their parents are raising them to be dependent. Maybe not by design, but in the long run that's what it will turn out to be. You have to raise your children to one day be able to fend for themselves. So it's important to teach them little stuff like doing their clothes, cooking, and when he gets older you show him how to, you know, balance a budget. . . . Even from the beginning, putting stuff up away from them so they won't break it. I never did that. I saw that as a learning tool. And even when they go to school, I think a sign of not teaching them how to be independent is not having them be responsible for their own actions. I see too many times parents, something happens at school, they want to come up and find out what was wrong. Like, for instance, if the school called and said Kyle was in a fight and they suspended him, I'm never going to ask what did they do with the other kid. I don't care. I want to deal with the issue—why he's fighting—when we get home. But we get parents who want to come in the school with six guns blazing. They are always coddling, making excuses. And then these same parents wonder why, when their kids get to be teenagers and young adults, why they keep coming back and can't seem to get on their feet. Parents are turning their children into victims.

Redmond couched independence in more pragmatic terms:

> You know, I tried to program my children: once you are eighteen, you are going somewhere. You know, when you get out of high school, I'm not taking care of grown people. You can go to college or in the service after high school, and there will be a room here for you during breaks. If you get a job, you are going to pay rent if you stay here or you need to look for your own place.

Kenneth and Raymond both defined independence in terms of intellectual freedom. Kenneth mentioned that his political views and voting behavior were determined by his dad. Until he was thirty, he just voted for whomever his dad told him to. Raymond, the minister's son, viewed independence in terms of freedom to choose one's own religious beliefs and values:

> That was something that I wanted to make sure—I don't believe in forcing religion on people, forcing them to believe something that you believe, simply because you believe it. So Tommy has not been baptized and it will not be my decision to have him baptized. Because I think that that has to be his choice, his belief, his faith in God. With my parents, I was forced to go to church, forced to do this or that. There was no option.

Despite the fact that many fathers said they didn't want too much obedience or unwavering civility or respect toward others, as with most parents, the absence of these behaviors elicited punishment. House rules that were broken, chores that were supposed to be done but were "forgotten" or, more likely, misbehaviors in school were the most frequent incidents that resulted in punishment of one sort or another. Aside from one teen daughter who had been adjudicated delinquent in juvenile court for drug use, most child infractions were minor, of the usual sort that most parents encounter.

How fathers dealt with these infractions, the disciplinary measures used, ran the gamut and at times were quite humorous to all involved, at least in hindsight. As is the case with most surveys of American parents (Schroeder 2008), the majority of fathers said they had used corporal punishment—spanking—at one time or another. Three fathers said they spanked fairly regularly, but five said they had never spanked. The majority used it on occasion but preferred to avoid it if possible. Several recounted being reared in a family where corporal punishment was used regularly on them and, by their own estimates, too severely and without positive results. Several spoke of beatings with belts and sticks and being hit on the face and head, resulting in welts and bruises. Jay had been spanked only once by his father and once by his mother, but his brother was spanked regularly with a strap. Jay said it didn't do any good; his brother was "as wild as he always was." So Jay has only used corporal punishment once with his oldest son, now in his early twenties:

> He did something; I forgot what it was. He was like twelve or thirteen. Whatever it was, it didn't warrant me putting my hands on him. Maybe it was the pressure of the time. After, I stopped and I thought about it. I thought, "I could really beat this kid. I can physically beat this kid. I've got more moves, my arms are longer." I had never done it before, and I lost it. I snapped and I did it that one time, and I gave him a good whomping, you know. By his being twelve or thirteen, he was pretty big and strapping. But I realized, "I could really knock the daylights out of this kid."

Consequently, although the majority used spanking on occasion, even they tended to set some constraining criteria—such as only hitting the buttocks or legs, only using the hand, and/or only when the misbehavior is dangerous or illegal—in the use of corporal punishment. For instance, Lanny, who has a noncustodial son and a custodial daughter, Emily, said he spanked his daughter for having forged his name on a school permission slip. He waited to spank until he had cooled down so that the spanking was planned and reasonable. He elaborated:

> I never whooped my son yet, but I did whoop Emily one time. [He describes the forging incident, which he learned of on a school morning]. I told her "we'll continue this when I get home." So after school, it was a Tuesday, Marcus [his son] was [at my house] too. I gave her the spanking on my bed, and I told Marcus he better not sign my name like that. It hurted me, you know. I gave her about five licks. I don't know if I was even hitting her hard. It hurted me to see her crying. I know, my mother never whooped me upside the head. That's when child abuse comes into play, if you discipline your child out of anger. Then you can't control how you swing. I had the whole day to calm down—I mean, maybe I would have given her some harder swings if I had done it right then and there.

James admitted that even if he wanted to use corporal punishment, he probably couldn't bring himself to do it. "As far as having to whoop them all, I don't do that," he admitted. "I don't even worry about that. When I get a belt, they laugh at me. They really do. I don't even get the belt; I just talk about it. . . . I'll say 'I'm going to get a belt.' And she'll say, 'come here and give me a kiss, dad.'"

So in their own turn as parents, most fathers relied on the withdrawal of privileges, particularly privileges that they knew their children love, such as television, movies, phone use, attending school dances, and socializing with friends. For instance, Kenneth disciplined his daughter for a bad report card. While he wanted to make the point that she needed to spend more time and effort on school work, he didn't want to diminish her play time because when she was living with her mother, she didn't have many physical activities and she is now overweight, so he withdrew television. He explains,

> I don't like to take away play time because we have the weight issue, so she's gonna go outside and play. She needs to be outside and play. When the report card came out, her grades had dropped really low, so TV time was suspended pretty much until I got reassurance from her teacher that her grades had come back up, and that ended up being about three weeks. Pretty much she watched no TV, and the only video she was allowed to watch was School House Rock.

However, some fathers created unusual alternatives to corporal punishment and withdrawal of privileges. Billy reminisced about strategies that he tried when his kids were younger; he complains that often these strategies punished him as well.

> My kids have never been hit, never been spanked. We had some dumb punishments. My main thing was I would make them go to bed on a Friday. Now a lot of kids would recognize this as a great thing, but when you go to bed on a Friday, no music, no TV, no reading, you just in the bed. Saturday you'd get up and eat and go right back to bed. Come Saturday afternoon and night, you laying in there and then you can't go back to sleep. That's when it starts getting rough. . . . Sometimes I would leave home for half an hour so that they could get up and do whatever, but I found that I was putting myself on punishment as well, cuz I had to stay in and watch them.

While Dominic described his methods of punishment to me, his teenaged son Tony sat nearby listening. Dominic explained, "I used to use the corner hand rotation thing, but it's been a long time." I looked inquisitively, and Tony graciously described the method: "you go in the corner, and put your arms out to your sides and make small circles till your arms get tired." Dominic continued: "And that's pretty good punishment for young kids. Then there's running in place; there's carrying the books above the head. I had a thousand and one tortuous ones. I'd give them some off-the-wall number that I knew they weren't going to accomplish, like 1,000 jumping jacks. After about 20, I'd say 'Oh, you missed one. Start over.' I'd do that about three times in a row, and then he'd start crying and I'd say 'do you think you learned a little?'" Tony and his Dad are laughing together at this point.

Rubin referred to his preferred discipline tactic as "humming," by which he meant a type of nagging.

> I'm the kind of parent that is just always like a humming in your ear, if you're doing something wrong. I know a humming in the ear can be almost as irritating as someone screaming. I say to him, "I can see you are upset with it, but if you are really upset about it, you'll stop doing it because you don't want to hear me say it again. I'm not going to scream at you about it." But the point I try to make with him is that if you dislike the hum, get on the stick, get with it.

Raymond, who was one of those who looked to Bill Cosby and Felicia Rashad in the *Cosby Show* as role models for parenting, said he liked to incorporate a little sarcastic humor to drive home the point. He gave this example of how he dealt with his son Tommy's misbehavior in first grade when he had just started going to a new school. Tommy, who was adopted at age three from foster care, had called his kindergarten teacher a "bitch" several times in class. Raymond recalls,

> So finally I asked him, "What's her name?" He said the teacher's name, and I said, "Are you sure? Sure it's not 'bitch'?" He said, "No, it's Mrs. Smith," and I said "Maybe her first name is 'bitch.'" And he said, "No, no." I said, "I know, you weren't talking to her. Maybe there was someone standing behind her, and her name was 'bitch.'" So, you know, I just made a big deal that one time. He knew I was not happy about this. And he hasn't done it since. Even when he has heard the word on TV since then, he said, "They said the b-word."

I asked fathers whether "time-outs" were part of their discipline regimen. Although some of the dads said they used time-outs, Theo indicated time-outs in and of themselves were too bland. He said, "Putting your kid on a time-out—that's not discipline. [Discipline] is explaining what you did wrong, trying to make her think about positive choices, what she could have done differently, being consistent." Jay agreed; he preferred to tailor the punishment to fit the crime.

> I tried to be more creative than time-outs. Time-out is good; it works; it's like the first step. But there was never just a time-out and that's it. There was always a time-out until I think about the severity of what you've done, and then comes the "punishment."

To illustrate, Jay went on to tell the story of how his daughter and a male friend of hers found a wallet with a credit card. Instead of turning it in or notifying the owner, they headed to Toys R Us, where they spent about $600. His daughter came home and told him that she had done something "really wrong." The way Jay handled it illustrated his desire to wear multiple hats and balance the various parental roles. He recounts,

> Now I knew I had to discipline her but I also had to be her friend. Because I wanted her to be able to come back to me if something else happened in the future. If I had jumped all over her . . . if I had been disciplinarian first, I think I would have lost that friendship that we had and that trust that friends have. So I took them back [to the store] and made her confess, and I went over to the parents' house of the boy and told them what I was going to do. The police got involved and it was worked out where they were able to take back most of the stuff. There were a few things they weren't [able to take back], and she had to pay it back. So that was the teaching part. Then what about the discipline? Taking it back is not the discipline; taking it back is part of realizing you made a mistake and you're asking for forgiveness and you're willing to work

and do whatever they want. Do I get a belt and beat people? I'm not a beater. So I had her write a letter of apology to all the people she hurt and to the school newspaper. So I believe that even though she did that crime, I believe that the fact that all the other things that I set up in her life by us being friends makes her able to come to me and tell me. I may be way out in left field, but that's the way I've always felt.

Jay seemed oblivious to the fact that his daughter's confession of her crime to him in the first place was evidence that his disciplining methodology—balancing what seem to be two contrary roles of disciplinarian and friend—had already been successful, as she herself had confessed the wrongdoing.

Finally, a few of the fathers mentioned that they used preventive strategies to head off unwanted behaviors. Usually they meant closely monitoring their children's interactions. For example, Antoine doesn't allow his daughter to attend any sleepovers or parties unless he knows the parents. James monitors his daughters' interactions with boys, telephone calls, and computer use. He describes his strategy:

> I've talked to Bonnie—she's fifteen—and say "you're not old enough to date, and I would prefer you not even get into it." Well, I don't know what she does at school. I can't speak on that, but I do know that no one calls the house, no boys. She has her own cell phone. No one calls that because I monitor a lot of the calls that she gets, and it's definitely not no boys. She loves the computer; sometimes she be on that. She goes to different websites, and I had to stop her from that. Some guy sent her . . . I don't know what happened. One day I sat down to my computer to do something, maybe just check my e-mails, and all of a sudden I get an eight-page printout. Some guy was asking a lot of crazy questions about is she having sex, is she dating. So I started reading this thing, and I just reached in the computer drawer and got a paper clip, put it together and threw it in the drawer so that when she got home that afternoon, I confronted her with this. And I said, "You are not going on the computer no more until I think you are ready to go on there." I said, "some of those websites are not for you." I have parental guidance on there and a lock. I don't know how she got on that website. . . . And like I said, some things I just discipline her by just stopping her from doing the things she wants to do, and she'll cooperate very good with me.

Conclusion

In sum, the roles that these single fathers prioritize—primarily provider and nurturer—would not be unexpected because those two roles are most prevalent in the cultural lingo and, like most everyone, fathers draw upon the familiar cultural repertoire of parenthood. In particular, as single parents they feel they must supply what have traditionally been viewed as both the male (provider) and female (nurturer) roles. The lesser importance placed on authority figure and disciplinarian would seem congruent with their emphases on nurturer, as other studies show that fathers who choose the authoritarian role tend to be less involved parents (Gaertner et al. 2007). Hence, it would be logical that these very involved fathers reject an authoritarian role for the most part. However, the downplaying of the friend role would not seem congruent with the emphasis on nurturer. A possible interpretation is that fathers viewed "friend" as the polar opposite of "authority figure" and did not desire either extreme to predominate in their parenting style. One might also speculate that the fathers' choice of roles could be influenced indirectly by the characteristics of the custodial child or directly by advice straight from the child's mouth. For instance, the two fathers with children who were experiencing some behavioral problems listed "authority figure" in the top two most important positions. These suggest that certain types of children may more likely elicit certain parental roles. It certainly suggests that parenting style is negotiated between parent and child, rather than something that is simply chosen by an autonomous parental decision. In the next chapter I will explore the possible role that the gender of their children might have played in the way these fathers viewed their parenting experience.

The results also indicated a general consensus on the behavioral expectations fathers had for their children. All of the fathers held high behavioral expectations for their children, and educationally speaking all expected that their children would go on to college. Independence and self-reliance, the ability to support themselves, seemed to be the goals most sought after. Creativity, getting along with others, and willing to try new things were the least desirable (though not undesirable), perhaps because they seemed to be the ones most likely to support behavioral deviance and yielding to peer pressure. Even the preferred expectations of obedience and respect for authority were desired in moderation, likewise with the hope of preventing their children from following stronger personalities or authority figures into unsafe or self-defeating situations.

In terms of role models and other sources of role definition and advice, it was generally found that the fathers' mothers were the primary source of positive symbolic meaning and advice, while their fathers were least. The fact that the men saw themselves largely in terms of providing and nurturing indicates that they observed and modeled these after their mothers, who themselves had often performed both roles, and/or that these roles are driven largely by a "viscerally felt absence" of those characteristics in their own fathers. Other sources, such as the media and the Internet, while used infrequently for parenting role models and advice, were still cited more than parenting books or support groups. Whether this is an increasing trend for all parents of our technological age or whether black single fathers, in particular, find these venues more tolerable than others would be a question for future researchers to pursue.

While the small size and self-selected nature of this sample of fathers prohibit generalization beyond this group of fathers, the main conclusion drawn is that these fathers were indistinct from most other parents in the roles they play and the goals they have for their children. The wide variation among them, in defining independence and in discipline methods, for instance, should illustrate that black single fathers, even though a relatively small group, are not a monolith. Their parental roles are multifaceted and perhaps adaptive to the particular child and over time. Like most parents, they are learning as they go, feeling their way through each developmental stage, and balancing competing goals. They see parenting as a process of guiding and teaching, with the goal of ultimately producing a child who will be productive in society, able to live life fully after their parents' obligations have been met, and who will make them feel that it was, in the end, worth it.

CHAPTER FOUR

Fathering Daughters and Sons
The Role of the Child's Gender

Dominic grew up in a single-mother household in a mid-sized midwestern city. He saw his dad, an alcoholic, very irregularly. At eighteen his high school sweetheart, a white woman, became pregnant with his child. Although his family was more accepting of the relationship than hers, neither side was thrilled to see them together. So after high school he entered the military, and his girlfriend went to live with his sister during the pregnancy and birth of their son, Tony. When Dominic left the military, he and his girlfriend, Staci, and son moved in to their own apartment, but after a while Staci took Tony and left to a southern state. In order to be with Tony, Dominic followed them, and they eventually moved in together again and married. During the next couple years, Staci had an affair with a white man and became pregnant. Dominic left and moved in with a friend back in their home state. Shortly after the birth of a daughter Jiji, Staci asked to reunite, and so Dominic traveled south and moved her and the two children back north with him. They had their third child, another daughter, Marcia, during this reunion. Right before Marcia's birth, Dominic underwent a kidney transplant, which his body rejected, and he became very sick. During this critical time, his wife took the girls and left. Two days later she returned and left the girls with Dominic who was being nursed back to health by his mother and eleven-year-old Tony. Dominic recovered and today works at a women's center. At the time of the interview, he had reared his three children alone for four years. Staci lives in the same city and has visitation rights, plus she has another son from a new boyfriend. Dominic claimed this fourth child on his insurance until he could prove this child was not his.

Cameron's parents divorced when he was two, and he didn't see his dad again until he was 18. Cameron had his two children with a girlfriend during an on-again, off-again relationship, starting when they were both eighteen. His girl-friend had custody of the children at first, but one New Year's Eve she left the children with a friend while she stayed out all night. The friend called the po-lice, who called Cameron, who was living with his mom. Cameron took cus-tody of the son immediately, but he had yet to go through paternity proceedings for the daughter, so she was placed in foster care for three months while Cameron's paternity was adjudicated. Initially, Cameron only had placement of the children, not legal custody. During the three years of placement, Cameron cashed two fraudulent checks, just enough to be classified as a felony, and went off to a Huber facility for nine months, while the children re-mained with his mom. Because a Huber facility allows inmates to work, he was able to remain the primary provider for his children, and the court awarded him legal custody. At the time of the interview, he had had placement and custody seven years. Since being out of prison he has had trouble finding stable, full-time employment. Although he has worked since he was thirteen years old, at the time of the interview he was employed as a janitor about twenty-five hours a week and was trying to become a real estate appraiser. He cohabits with a new girlfriend, with whom he has had twin sons, six months old at the time of the interview. His girlfriend, who also has one son from a previous relationship, works full-time while Cameron does most of the care for the five children. As Cameron and I talk, the three older children play at the kitchen table, and Cameron sits on the living room floor rocking the snoozing twins. They live in a small apartment in a neighborhood displaying many boarded windows. Cameron's frustration with his inability to secure stable em-ployment is palpable, and he hints that his current girlfriend is not too happy about it either. The mother of his two older children pays irregular child sup-port, totaling about $1,000 a year.

Traditionally, much research on fathers and their children reflects the pre-sumption that men and boys are naturally closer and that single fathers, if they had their druthers, would prefer custody of boys over girls. And for the most part, the findings do support these presumptions. Co-resident dads tend to be more involved with sons than daughters (Harris, Furstenberg, Morgan and Allison 1987; Harris and Morgan 1991; Starrels 1994; Updegraff et al. 2001), and with few exceptions noncustodial fathers also spend more time with and are closer to sons than to daughters (Cooksey and Craig 1998; Furstenberg, Nord, Peterson, and Zill 1983). From the child's perspective, Manning and Smock (1999) and King (2002) find that among nonresident and divorced dads, sons report more frequent visits with and more emotional closeness to fathers than do daughters. Likewise, sons in early and mid-adolescence also report significantly greater emotional closeness and behavioral involvement with married fathers than do daughters (Youniss and Smollar 1985).

In general, most previous studies (Cancian and Meyer 1998; Chang and Deinard 1982; Fox and Kelly 1995; Grief 1985, 1990; Hanson 1988; Ihinger-Tallman et al. 1995; Marsiglio 1991; Morgan, Lye, and Condran 1988) of single custodial fathers indicate that fathers are more likely to take custody of boys than girls. And as indicated in chapter 1, national census data uphold this finding. Both single dads and single moms have a greater preponderance of same-sex custodial children. Specifically, in Greif's 1985 survey of 1,136 single custodial dads, 42 percent were raising sons only, 27 percent were raising daughters only, and 31 percent were raising both. Hanson's 1988 study found 57 percent of the fathers had custody of boys only, and 43 percent had custody of girls only. Perhaps this gendered pattern of custody occurs because mothers of boys press for more father involvement and/or because mothers are more willing to relinquish sons to fathers. In any case, it came as some surprise, then, that those specific trends were not reflected in this sample.

The present group of fathers, though not necessarily representative of black single custodial fathers as a whole, contradict expectations that as single fathers they would have custody mostly of boys. These twenty dads had a total of thirty-seven custodial children, and 60 percent were daughters. Of the twenty households, nine had only daughters (twelve girls total), four had only sons (four boys total), and seven had both boys and girls (twenty-one children total).

Recent research has begun to highlight the effect of dads on their daughters, but the outcomes investigated are often traditionally gendered, such as looking at the effects fathers have on daughters' "promiscuity," weight, and self-esteem. Coney and Macky (1997) found that father presence during the formative years is a deterrent to promiscuity, which they measured using rates of nonmarital births and sexually transmitted diseases. Harris et al. (1998) found that daughters whose fathers have warm close relationships with them and spend time with them in shared activities were less likely to engage in early sexual activity. Dominy, Johnson, and Koch (2000) found that obese women with binging disorders perceive their fathers as more rejecting than do other women and more rejecting than they perceive their moms. Not surprisingly, Scheffler and Naus (1999) found a positive relationship between father involvement and daughter's self-esteem.

A few earlier studies have specifically investigated children's outcomes based on same-sex custody. For instance, Santrock and Warshak (1979) found that father-custody boys were more socially competent than boys in two-parent families. By social competence, the researchers meant the boys scored higher on warmth, maturity, self-esteem, sociability, and depth. According to their study, father-custody girls scored lower on all of these measures. Guttman (1982) found a similar pattern; that is, that father-custody boys had better outcomes than father-custody girls. While the present study did not measure outcomes for children, one could speculate that fathers might be similarly impacted by same-sex custody, that is, they might rank lower on outcomes when custody is across genders.

Because the majority of the children in this study were legal minors and many of them very young, I limited my investigation to the fathers' perspectives on parenting of daughters and sons. Once I noticed the unexpected gendered household composition, I explored the data to see in what ways fathers of daughters saw their roles differently than did fathers of sons. Would their perceptions of self or of parenting vary? Although there was a range of answers among the individual fathers, aggregate patterns according to the child's gender were noteworthy.

In regard to satisfaction, the questionnaire asked fathers to indicate whether they felt "very satisfied," "somewhat satisfied," or "not too satisfied" with their parenting of each custodial child. In regard to emotional closeness, fathers were asked to indicate whether they felt "very close to," "somewhat close to," "not too close to," or "distant from" each of their custodial children. To get a sense for their frame of mind, fathers were given a list of twelve adjectives (seven negative and five positive) and were asked to pick three that best described how they perceived themselves. In regard to all three measures, a distinct gender difference surfaced again.

In regard to parenting satisfaction, as illustrated in table 4.A, daughter-only fathers were "very satisfied" with their parenting of only 42 percent of their daughters, whereas sons-only fathers were "very satisfied" in parenting 100 percent of their sons. Likewise, in terms of emotional proximity, daughters-only fathers felt very close to a slight majority (58 percent) of their daughters, whereas sons-only fathers felt "very close" to 100 percent of their sons. In mixed-children households, the results were oddly contradictory. In those households, fathers were more satisfied with their parenting of daughters than sons, but felt closer to their sons.

The pattern for self-descriptors was also gendered. Because each father was asked to pick three adjectives, the nine daughters-only fathers had a total of twenty-seven descriptors and the four sons-only fathers had a total of twelve. Despite the fact that the list of descriptors tilted toward the negative, the majority of the chosen descriptors were positive, but daughters-only fathers were slightly more likely than sons-only fathers to choose negative outcomes.

Table 4.A. Rankings of Satisfaction and Closeness

	% Very Satisfied	% Very Close
Daughters-only dads	42%	58%
Mixed-gender dads	33% overall	67% overall
	40% daughters	56% daughters
	25% sons	88% sons
Sons-only dads	100%	100%

One-third of the adjectives for daughters-only fathers were negative descriptors, such as "uncertain," "frustrated," "stressed," or "lonely." One-fifth of sons-only fathers' adjectives were negative.

Demographic or aggregate data frequently provide different perspectives of and explanations for various phenomena than do qualitative data, and it was no different here. According to the demographic data, several factors might help to account for the fathers' gendered parenting experience. The degree of choice that fathers had in regard to custody and the age and number of children in the household could have contributed to the lower levels of father satisfaction and emotional closeness to their daughters. Previous studies have found that father satisfaction is positively related to the degree of choice. Moreover, studies on marital dissatisfaction show that dissatisfaction is higher when there are more children (Plechaty et al. 1996) and when children are in their teen years (Steinberg and Silverberg 1987). Having only daughters also tends to lower marital satisfaction (Katzev, Warner, and Acock 1994). Hence, it's quite possible the presence of more and older children, as well as their gender, would have a similar effect on a single father.

As mentioned in chapter 2, choice is a difficult variable to measure. If we look to previous marital status as a measure of choice, we find that 75 percent of the sons-only fathers were never married, and one of them was an adoptive father. Thus, we could presume that the majority of these sons-only fathers were not legally obligated to take custody. This means that sons-only fathers were largely fathers who had more choice. The majority of daughters-only fathers were also unmarried, but the percentage is only two-thirds. One-third of them had been married before; two of the marriages resulted in divorce, one in widowhood. Divorced fathers were the least satisfied.

Daughters-only households were more likely to have two children in them, while all the sons-only households contained only one child. In fact, all the daughters-only households with two children were the households in which the father was divorced or widowed. The average age of the children in daughters-only households was ten years, but it was a little higher for those

whose fathers said they felt only somewhat close to their daughters and a little lower for those whose fathers said they felt very close to their daughters.
The average age in sons-only households was 6.5 years. Having more children and children in or near the teen years would likely affect both the level
of satisfaction and the degree of emotional closeness. Many parents attest to
the fact that the ages of five to preteen tend to be among the easiest childrearing years and that frequently both parents and teens tend to distance
themselves from one another during the teen years (Steinberg and Silverberg
1987). Fathers are known to distance themselves from daughters at puberty.
Most parents do to some extent, but fathers do so longer than do moms,
whose involvement with children does not differ significantly by sex of the
child (Videon 2005).

In addition to the above father outcomes, as mentioned in chapter 3, fathers were given a set of roles to rank in importance (one being most important, six being least important) to their identity as fathers. The set of roles
included provider, nurturer, teacher, friend, authority figure, and disciplinarian. A breakdown by child's gender (see tables 4.B and 4.C) shows some distinct differences in role importance. As with the above measures of satisfaction and closeness, I divided the fathers into those who had daughters only
(nine fathers with twelve daughters), sons only (four fathers with four sons),
or both (seven fathers with twenty-one children) and then compared the
daughter-only and son-only families. I reiterate that this small sample is not
generalizable, so the percentages given below are only intended to illustrate
noticeable patterns, not statistical significance.

Table 4.B. Rankings of Parental Roles for Fathers of Daughters Only

Father/# of daughters	Provider	Nurturer	Friend	Authority Figure	Teacher	Disciplinarian
Darren (2)	1	2	5	4	3	6
John (1)	2	1	5	6	4	3
Lanny (1)	1	2	6	5	4	3
Theo (1)	1	3	5	6	2	4
Calvin (1)	1	2	5	6	3	4
Kenneth (1)	1	3	6	4	5	2
Antoine (1)	1	2	4	6	3	5
James (2)	1	3	5	7	2	4
Conrad (2)	2	3	4	1	5	6
% ranked 1–2	100	56	7	11	22	11
% ranked 5–6	0	0	89	67	22	33

1 = most important   6 = least important

Table 4.C. **Rankings of Parental Roles for Fathers of Sons Only**

Father/# of sons	Provider	Nurturer	Friend	Authority Figure	Teacher	Disciplinarian
Rubin (1)	3	2	4	5	1	6
Angelo (1)	3	2	4	5	1	6
Raymond (1)	4	1	5	2	3	6
Tracy (1)	1	2	3	6	4	5
% ranked 1–2	25	100	0	25	50	0
% ranked 5–6	0	0	25	75	0	100

1 = most important   6 = least important

Fathers saw their parenting roles differently depending on the gender of their children. Especially noteworthy is that all of the daughters-only fathers ranked the "provider" role in first or second place of importance, while only one-fourth of the sons-only fathers saw themselves foremost as providers. Only 56 percent of daughters-only fathers saw themselves as nurturers, while all of the sons-only fathers ranked that in first or second importance. Remember from chapter 3 that, overall, "friend" was ranked low, but breaking it down by gender of child shows that the low ranking largely stems from the fathers of daughters, as nearly 90 percent of daughters-only fathers saw being a friend as low in importance, ranking it in fifth or sixth place, whereas only 25 percent of sons-only fathers viewed the friend role as low in importance. Disciplinarian was ranked largely at a middle level of importance by fathers of daughters, but fathers of sons all ranked it low. Fathers of sons only ranked teacher somewhat higher than did fathers of daughters only. The only role on which there was some agreement was "authority figure"; the majority of both sets of fathers ranked it low.

As to the gender differences on the provider role, one might speculate that the father-daughter relationship, more so than the father-son relationship, may replicate in the men's minds the traditional husband-wife relationship in which the husband is expected to provide for the wife. Or perhaps the fathers think that daughters are (or will be as they get older) more demanding consumers than are the sons. A couple of the fathers said that their children complained that they didn't buy them enough things, and both of these fathers had daughters. As you will see later, a couple more fathers complained about having to shop with their daughters. Perhaps it is not that fathers have to shop more with daughters, but at least they view the shopping experience as less enjoyable with girls.

Moreover, daughters-only households were much more likely to have higher income. About two-thirds of daughters-only households had incomes above $35,000; about 40 percent had above $50,000, whereas among sons-only households, none had above $35,000. From this limited data, it is unclear what the relationship between household income and the gender of the child is. It is unlikely that having daughters created more motivation for men to earn more money, as most of the income differences were in place prior to custody. More likely is that men with higher incomes were, for some reason, more likely to take custody of daughters. Divorced and widowed men are more likely to have higher incomes than never-married men, and one-third of daughters-only households were headed by such men. More noteworthy is that one would have expected the higher income to contribute to higher levels of satisfaction in daughter-only households, but apparently it could not outweigh other satisfaction-reducing factors. This leads us to the qualitative data, to the fathers' narratives themselves, for another source of explanation.

Qualitative: What the Fathers Say about Parenting Daughters—Seeking Gender Balance

A number of studies have suggested that gender roles are more egalitarian in black families than white families. These conclusions are largely based on the strong financial role black women have traditionally played in the black family; black women have historically had higher labor-force-participation rates than white women. Also, black men tend to hold less traditional attitudes toward women's employment and motherhood than do white fathers (Hofferth 2003). However, such attitudes may not necessarily transfer to how fathers rear their daughters, as men's expectations might differ for young girls compared to women or for one's daughter compared to one's wife or for one's own child compared to another's.

With few exceptions, when asked directly, most fathers said their behavioral expectations (addressed in chapter 3) would be the same for both sons and daughters. Rubin said he was trying to rear his son to be a human being, as opposed to a "man."

> Society wants to instill all those—quote, unquote—masculine labels, you know? Things you sort of do as a man. I put more emphasis on things he should do as a human being, as a person. Because his maleness and all, that's a given. And it may manifest itself in any number of ways. But he'll still be a man. Eventually, he'll be a man. I try not to—I stay away from the traditional attitudes of, you know, the man being in charge and the women are the subordinates. I constantly impress upon him that . . . it's an equal share thing. There are differences, but in any type of relationship or agreement or partnership or

anything like that, you got to draw from the things that you know and the things that they know and try to come together and get some type of happy medium, not go into a situation with all these ideas of "I'm in charge and you're not." . . . To me it's nonsense, because to me it's more detrimental to a successful relationship. You know, . . . I know guys who will go in and say, "well, I ain't doing no cooking, I ain't doing this, I ain't, I ain't, I ain't." Or, on the contrary, women who feel that certain things are man's work and this is women's work. For instance, I couldn't be in a relationship with a woman who said, "You stay out of my kitchen." That would rule her out. Those are the type of values that I try to instill in him. Whether or not when he becomes a man he is that way, who can say? But I feel as a parent that I'm giving him alternatives to other things.

Though Rubin was in the minority in articulating such an ideology, many of the men seemed to be attempting to treat their sons and daughters equitably, but found it difficult. A number of men said they themselves were reared with a "traditional" gender ideology and grew up doing "guy" chores, such as taking out the garbage and mowing the lawn. They often vacillated between this ideology and striving to treat their children equally. Billy, father of Otto, who is now in college, and Amelia, a high schooler, illustrates this conundrum. Although he wants to avoid differential treatment, in the end he concludes that only his daughter needs a woman around. He said,

I was [raised] by the age-old adage that a man's a man and a woman's a woman. But when I started looking at my kids the same and not placing any differential treatment, it worked out fine. I didn't look at him [Otto] as a man. I looked at him at first as a man, when I was telling him about his name, keep his name clean, [but] now it's the same for Amelia. As far as looking at my kids or weighing them any different, I don't. But I also recognize the fact that the only difference is that Amelia needs a woman in her life and Otto don't.

Some of the men feared they were failing their daughters in this respect, falling short of the social ideal of a mother and a father, or mother and father figures, in the same household. Calvin said,

[Not having a mother in the home] has always been a factor; it's always been something I've had to struggle with. It's always something I feel guilty about, that . . . just I feel guilty about, you know, the fact that there was just a situation that I and her mother couldn't work out. And now, she has to choose between . . . she can't have a mother and a father there. That's always bothered me.

Sometimes this guilt is generated or exacerbated by comments outsiders make. Several fathers said that other people—friends, coworkers, family members—had suggested that a woman could do a better job. After all, people often presume that women turn a house into a home, invest more energy to improve relations, and are better caretakers. Part of this stems from the idea that men and women have essential differences that render them complementary, each having characteristics the other lacks, one supplying the yin, the other the yang, so to speak. Antoine illustrates,

> I think [having a woman in the house] would help because it would bring balance, you know the father figure and then the woman figure in the house. . . . She [the daughter] could bounce ideas off both of us and sometimes you need that . . . you don't always need the testosterone in the house. Sometimes you need estrogen . . . you need the woman's point of view.

But only fathers of daughters expressed this need for gender balance or the assumption that children need the presence of the *same-sex* parent, which is not equivalent to the idea that both sons and daughters need exposure to both genders of parents. While several fathers said their sons needed them as a "father figure," none suggested their sons also needed a mother figure. At least three of the dads who have boys expressed the idea that a boy needs a man. Despite the fact that sons-only fathers ranked "authority figure" low, this idea was often associated with a boy's need for authority, the presumption that a boy will more likely obey his father than his mother. Tracy, father of Train, said:

> I wanted to be there, you know, because—his mother hates to admit this—but I tell him to do something, he does it. She'll tell him, he'll do it, but he'll take his time about it. She'll have to tell him two or three times. And I don't think you should have to do that with no child. Just by having that male figure there, and having somebody who really loves you and cares about you—I see it in my son all the time. When I was nine years old, I was getting into things. I can leave him alone in this house for maybe an hour or two, and I come back to the house and the house is still the same. He won't do nothing.

Angelo, who has custody of his infant son, emphasized the teaching role that he could play for his son. If he waited until his son was older to take custody, he feared he would not be able to deter him from habits and lifestyles that many young boys are exposed to. Anthony explained:

> I would just say that a lot goes on in a lot of families; our kids grow up so fast. And to be a parent, you just have to start from day one, to get them off on the

right track. I figured no one could do this better than his father. . . . I could teach him things, if you start having somebody while they're young, instead of taking him when he gets older.

On the other hand, for fathers of daughters the concern over the lack of a mother figure was not associated with discipline; rather it was more associated with the need for a nurturer, friend or teacher. As mentioned earlier, fathers who had girls only or both girls and boys were more likely to rank nurturing slightly lower (no one ranked it in the two least important positions) than those who had boys only, and fathers of daughters were more likely to view nurturing as a quality found more in women than in men. For instance, Ronald, custodial father for twelve years of Jet, his sixteen-year-old son, and Carla, his fourteen-year-old daughter, spoke openly:

I guess I wasn't built for some of the stuff that happened. I guess I'm saying that some women I feel are built to be more nurturing, to be more sensitive, to be more loving to her children. Whereas as a man I felt like I was as nurturing and as loving as I felt I could be. But at the same time I don't feel that I was quite as . . . nurturing and sensitive with my daughter. I felt that raising her, I didn't give her what she needed.

While the difference between fathers of sons and fathers of daughters was small in regard to the nurturing role, Ronald's statement may indicate that fathers of daughters felt, rightly or wrongly, that daughters require a different degree or kind of nurturing than sons, a type that they as fathers could not fulfill or a type they are not comfortable giving. Ronald's concern that he was unable to give his daughter what she needed will be echoed later by other fathers.

Virtually all of the men viewed their own mothers as nurturing and hoped that they could draw upon that experience as a model for their own parenting. Kenneth, who was reared in a two-parent family, associates nurturing with love, self-esteem building, and a concentration on relationships, which he received from his mom. When asked to define nurturing, he said,

That goes back to things that I said about my mom as actually having a relationship and everything with other people. I think that a big part of it comes from the nurturing that a child gets, you know, providing it, love, um, how you express love to another person, how you build someone back up when things don't go well and things like that. I think that is very important for a child. I think that's an important thing for a parent to do for a child so the child feels pretty protected, feels safe, feels that sense of love and everything. . . . If you don't get that in your home, I think that's important as far as friendship, marriage, you know anything like that.

He elaborated, giving an example of how he has nurtured his daughter of whom he's had custody eleven months. Note that his definition of nurturing involves being honest and forthright about problems, not shielding the daughter from criticism.

> When she came to stay, she had these issues from her previous school. I really think that her self-esteem was low. A lot of times she would just call me out of the blue and ask me "Daddy do you think I am fat? Daddy do you think I am dumb?" These are obviously labels that someone has dropped on her one time or another. She struggled with this. I would say, "Look, I know that you are a bright child. I talked to you all the time. I know the things that you know that most children don't know. I know things that you learned how to do at an early age; tie the shoes, things like that. I know that you are not dumb. Fat? You can stand to lose some weight, but it's okay because you will go outside and play and you will lose the weight." Just little things to assure her that there is nothing wrong with her and she is not inferior to any other kids at school. She knew she was making bad grades, so I told her, "look, you are making bad grades. You haven't been to school, and you can't make good grades without being at school. I'm going to make sure that you get to school every day. . . ." Just physically and mentally give her a pat on the back. Everything will be okay and to me that's nurturing. That's what I got from my mom.

Most of the fathers, regardless of their children's sex, included a show of love and affection in their definition of nurturing. But when gender entered the conversation, a few fathers made a distinction in the type or degree of affection. For instance, Tracy, custodial father of nine-year-old Train, explained:

> I think you must nurture kids. I mean, they always need that affection, tell them that you love them. I tell him everyday I love him. That's part of me nurturing him. I hug him before he goes to school. I hug him when he goes to bed. You know, give him a kiss on the cheek. He kiss me on the cheek. And that's something I want, you know, until one of us dies. Because just because you are men don't mean—they have to get out of that stereotype that men don't do those things. There's nothing wrong with that. I want to let him know that. Of course, I wouldn't kiss him on the lips, but the cheek is fine. That's fine.

Tracy feels the need to clarify that his physical affection for a son is limited by social conventions that frown upon two men kissing on the lips. Similarly, Theo, father of a two-year-old daughter, suggested that if he had a son he would probably show less affection than he does to his daughter, even though he says he tries not to overprotect her, letting her run and bump without running to her side every time she gets hurt. Nevertheless, he says: "I don't think I'd be as affectionate with her if she were a boy. I don't know why, but you know I give her little kisses and hugs all the time. I don't think I'd do that as much if she were a boy."

Puberty and Other "Girl Stuff"

The age of the girls makes a difference as well. Frequently when girls were young, it was assumed they'd be easier to rear. When Jay's wife died, his sisters said they couldn't rear the boys, but they were willing to take the daughter. Jay decided to keep them all together and rear them himself. In Dominic's case his ex-wife wanted custody of their girls but not the son. As mentioned in his vignette at the beginning of this chapter, when Dominic's ex-wife left, she took the two daughters and left their son Tony. Shortly thereafter, however, she returned the girls to Dominic as well. Even today for visitation, Tony, Dominic's son, says, "there's been times when I come home, a little bit later than the girls, from school. [My mom] wouldn't even wait; she'd just leave. She'd come get the girls and not even ask me if I want to go. She just assumes I want to be with my dad. Or she buys them clothes, but not me."

However, down the line, puberty complicates the situation for fathers; this is about the time fathers begin to think boys are easier to raise. Echoing the concerns about girls, Kenneth said: "[Now] I think that raising a boy would be easier. You know just on the basis of being able to relate better. Being [my daughter] is and soon will be going through things that I won't be able to relate to. I just won't be able to relate to the things, the physical and emotional changes, you know, whatever a little girl goes through."

What was very salient in their narratives is that fathers of daughters felt they were unable (or feared they would be unable in the future) to supply the friendship and teaching that they assumed a mother could provide. Frequently heard was the phrase that they wouldn't be able to "relate" to or "understand" their daughters' experience. The fact that men don't experience what women experience, primarily menstruation or "periods," makes them feel inadequate to meet their daughters' developmental needs. And, for the fathers, their daughters' menstruation is inextricably linked together with concerns about boys, dating, and sex. For instance, Calvin, the father of an eleven-year-old girl, says,

I don't know [chuckles] . . . I mean, as a male I don't know what women go through when they go through puberty. But I know they go through something and so just, you know, just dealing with boys and the period and talking about sex and you know, coming into her own as a young woman. I went through . . . I developed as a young man so I can't give her those, some of those, things. You know, I can love her and be affectionate and all, but there are still things that I'm sure she may not feel comfortable talking to me about or just things that I'm just not going to be able to relate to.

Like Calvin, Kenneth sees his nine-year-old daughter's puberty on the horizon and anticipates potential problems.

I'm not looking forward to when she starts liking boys. Right now she is kinda indifferent to 'em. She just sees them as peers. The soccer team she plays on is co-ed, and she prefers playing with little girls because she can get them to jump rope and stuff like that. They will play with dolls and stuff like that, but other than that, she is still pretty much indifferent. She'll go out and ride her bike and play kickball with 'em. I'm actually not looking forward to dating, but I'm assuming that's a good, good, good, good ways off in the future. . . . The period thing—that probably won't be a great time for me, but really just the dating thing is probably one of the things I'm dreading the most.

It wasn't just fear of conflict or not being able to understand one another. Many of the dads of daughters also said they regretted that they would not be able to *do* the things that they assume mothers do with their daughters, such as playing dress-up and putting on makeup. Darren, the father of two girls, said:

I worry about not having a mother or female figure in the home for them to learn from. I will never be able to talk to them about what it is like growing up as a lady—from a lady's point of view. How do I talk to them about periods in a way that they'll understand? I can't play dress up like they will want to do.

Clothes shopping was a frequent activity that fathers dreaded and avoided when possible. James, the father of two teen girls, admits that

the worst thing I do is go shopping with the girls. Oh my god! Oh my god! I bet I sit in front of the dressing room about an hour, or longer, for the big girl. The little girl, we can go shopping for her. I don't care where we go, . . . we can be in Boston Store or J.C. Penney's, anywhere; it doesn't take her long. She's "Dad, I know I like this. Can we get it?" And I say, "Yes, let's get the right size." But the big girl's gotta go to the dressing room, try it on, come out, see how she look. "Oh no, I don't want this. I gotta go try on another one." And, oh my goodness. A lot of times I send the big sister [a daughter from a previous relationship] with her. I just give them the money and tell her "you shop with her. I don't like [the mall] no way."

Kenneth also pointed to the shopping experience as one that was a bit problematic. He relayed the story of buying his daughter's first bra. After Sara slept over at her cousins, Kenneth's sister pulled him aside and said it was about time to buy his daughter some bras.

> So we went to Wal-Mart and, you know, we got the little training bras, . . . and she is not really to that point but she is a little bit overweight so she has extra flesh on her chest and everything, so she has to wear the little training bras.

Asked if it was embarrassing for him, he at first said no it was just something that had to be done, but then he remembered that the sales clerk turned out to be a former schoolmate. "There was one embarrassing incident because a guy that I went to school with was checking us out one day, and when we came through . . . he looked at me and looked at the bras and started laughing."

The frequency of these types of comments among fathers of girls likely helps to explain why "friend" and "teacher" were ranked lower in importance among girls-only fathers than among boys-only fathers. Although a few of the daughters participated in sports, many of the fathers still felt that there were gender-specific activities and topics that the fathers could not fully or equally participate in or comprehend. Because friendship frequently connotes intimacy, mutuality and empathy, these fathers may feel that, at best, they can attain only a limited friendship with their daughters.

Creating Independent Daughters

Fathers here exhibited some seemingly contradictory attitudes. On one hand, most fathers wanted their daughters to be strong and independent—emotionally and financially. On the other hand, many of them held more traditional ideas about girls being "ladylike" in their behavior. In her 1997 study, Jennifer Hamer found that African American noncustodial fathers were amenable to their daughters playing sports and going to games, but they also wanted their daughters to sit with legs closed; not wear makeup, jewelry, or short skirts; wear their hair long; and not hang out with "street" friends. In this study, John, father of a three-year-old daughter, was already concerned that his daughter wasn't learning a feminine role. "It's hard for a man to teach a girl how to be a lady. And it's things that she even has learned or is learning now that should be taught or would be taught by a woman." Likewise, Calvin said of his preteen daughter,

> One of the things that I was concerned about was her . . . I wanted her to act.
> . . . I would tell her to, you know, "you're a young lady now." There are certain things you shouldn't do, there are certain ways . . . you, know, there's a certain way you need to carry yourself, conduct yourself, and she didn't do that. And I thought well maybe if she's with her mother, maybe her mother could

do a better job of instilling those kinds . . . because she could have her mother to model off of. She doesn't see me in the bathroom putting on makeup or, you know, she may see me sitting around and, you know, just acting like a guy. So I began to be concerned about things like that . . . not being so tomboyish. I thought maybe she should have been a little more concerned about her appearance and her behavior. . . . I wasn't concerned about her wearing tight clothes and any of those because those kinds of clothes weren't being bought for her, not while she was with me. But even still, I'm even more concerned about, sometimes she would just, I just felt like she didn't care enough about her appearance. So I would begin to be concerned about her self-esteem.

However, as mentioned in chapter 3, fathers viewed independence as a desirable behavioral trait. Congruent with Baumrind's 1972 study of black fathers in two-parent families, fathers of daughters were as likely as fathers of sons to value independence. However, for fathers of daughters, having strong and independent daughters was very much tied to their concern that their daughters avoid being victims of men. Fathers minimally wanted their daughters to be free from financial, mental, and emotional dependence on men. For instance, when speaking of the characteristics he desired for his daughter Emily, Lanny said,

I want all that for my children. I want kindness, creative, polite, and compassion. I do want them to succeed academically and financially. I want—especially for my daughter—I want her to be independent. I don't want her to be dependent on a man. Because lots of women are dependent on a man.

Echoing the same thought, Jay said,

See, the number one thing that I really want to teach her . . . I mean she can go to school and learn ABCs and 1, 5, 7, . . . but what I want to teach her is to be able to be a woman and think for herself. I do not want a daughter that has to depend on a . . . I shouldn't say a "male," but that's what I mean . . . or anyone to do for her. I don't want my daughter growing up thinking, "I got to get married" or that "I gotta have a roommate." I want her to be stronger than that, to be able to make decisions for herself and make good decisions and be able to stand behind her decisions.

Dominic, who has two young daughters and an older son, expressed the worry that daughters could be victimized by men or could turn themselves into sexual objects of men.

I'm pretty concerned about my girls. I'm worried about some bum, toothless bum, just being mean to my girls. It looks like [my son] Tony already has some trampy girls. One of them had her bellybutton pierced. She was showing it to me and I was thinking, "'why would you want to show it to me?" No home training.

Dads under Suspicion

Fathers also indicated that rearing daughters had an impact on how the fathers themselves were perceived as well. Many men in traditionally female occupations or roles, such as daycare provider or elementary school teacher, have noted that they must face parental suspicions about why a male would want to work with children and must take more precautions than their female counterparts to preempt suspicion and accusation (Williams 1992).

These stereotypes constrain the parenting role for single dads. Billy, dad of a teen girl, said that one reason he worries about talking openly with his daughter about sex and bodily care is that others will wonder if he's abusing his daughter. He laments,

I know she needs a woman in her life. I know. You know, because in this day and age, people will get the wrong impression. You know, she tells people, her teachers, and [they ask] how does she know some of the stuff that she knows [about hygiene, shaving, menstruation, or sex]. And [she says] "my dad tells me," you know, and right then in this day and age, radar goes up. It truly does.

A couple other fathers suggested that it was difficult to arrange play dates and sleepovers for their daughters. Other parents would allow the single fathers' daughters to come to their house for a sleepover, but were reticent to allow their own daughters to sleep at the single dads' homes. Dominic held that his biggest parenting hurdle had been

finding play dates. Honestly, that's what I bump into. [Other parents] feel more comfortable with other women watching their children. When they find out you're a single man, and you're going to be keeping their children overnight, they get leery. Are you a pedophile? So play dates have been the biggest hassle.

Role of Mothers and Other Mothers

This suspicion, combined with the fathers' feelings of inadequacy as a nurturer, friend, and teacher as well as their concerns for their daughters' futures, often leads to the fathers looking to other women, "other mothers," for their daughters, something fathers of sons don't feel the same need to do. Greif's 1990 study of white single fathers similarly found that some fathers indicated discomfort with daughters' sexuality and sought outside female aid in discussing sex and hygiene. Hence, fathers took a number of strategies to accomplish this.

Many of the daughters visited their mothers on weekends, and the fathers often assumed or hoped that discussions about menstruation and sex were taking place at those times. Lanny, whose daughter is eleven, said he's uncomfortable talking about all those linked topics—the body, sex and dating. Although he plans to get to those conversations in the future, he's also hoping those conversations are occurring during the daughter's weekly visits to her mom's:

> I haven't talked to her about sex or anything like that. . . . I haven't brought that up yet. I feel kind of uncomfortable about that. Her mother can talk to her about it. Starting her period, washing herself and stuff. I haven't gone into detail at all. I always tell her, take a shower every morning and make sure you change your underwear. That's as far as I've went. Hate to say it, but I don't feel as comfortable talking about the period and the cleaning. . . . As far as the sex stuff, you know, I'm going to let her know. I'm going to talk to her. I'm not going to try to tell her she can't, . . . but I really just don't want her to start dating until she is sixteen. And I don't want her to go all the way till eighteen or nineteen.

A few fathers had girlfriends they could turn to. Antoine had his girlfriend deal with the menstruation topic. When his daughter was in fifth grade, Antoine received a notice from the school that they would be having a sex education class. Antoine commented,

> I was like—whoa! Fifth grade? I guess it's a good idea to talk to them young because that is when they start noticing things, but we talked about this stuff . . . some of the menstrual stuff, because it is going to happen sooner or later. Her cousin was here last summer and she got hers and I was like "Wow. Oh my god." My girlfriend was here and she was able to deal with all that stuff, so I was like "This ain't cool." I don't want to talk about it because she probably wouldn't feel comfortable talking to me about it anyways.

But some fathers did not have family or girlfriends, so they sought role models, confidantes, and mentors for their daughters among women in their communities, workplaces, or churches. Jay had his friend Kay give his daughter the sex talk. But seeking help from other women can come with attendant problems. Billy, a fifty-eight-year-old widower, lamented that some of the women he approached to be mentors for his daughter either wanted to also be romantically involved with him or thought he desired that.

> Now as far as being supportive [for my daughter], I'm going to be truthful. I haven't found the right people to do some of the things that I want to be done because to find people who can talk to my daughter is hard. Good intentions, but for somebody who just wants to take her under her wing, without me having to go through the romantic stage . . . it's hard."

A few fathers were hoping to marry, but some who weren't that anxious to enter another marriage were considering doing so just to put a woman in the home. Dominic works at a women's nonprofit agency and gets advice from his female coworkers. When he mentioned to the agency director that he had thought about asking his mother to move in, she told him his "kids would benefit from having a woman in the house." That made him think that remarriage might be the answer, particularly as he contemplates his daughters' future pubescence.

> My girls *are* getting bigger and . . . I don't know. They're still little; they're still daddy's little girls. But soon it will become more of an issue, and if I marry Jan [his girlfriend], it'll be solved. They love Jan to pieces, the girls do.

However, his son, Tony, does not care for Jan, who has two daughters of her own, foreshadowing an unfavorable household gender ratio in Tony's future. Dominic himself has mixed feelings about his girlfriend, but he may succumb to societal pressure to supply a "mother figure." For now, he thinks the girls are young enough that a dad is sufficient, but as with other dads, he sees puberty around the corner, and marriage might be the solution.

Puberty was a pivotal developmental stage that ignited thoughts about whether the daughter should be with her mother. Though most did not implement those thoughts, one father, Calvin, who had had custody of his daughter two separate times, totaling five years, had just returned his daughter who was nearing puberty to her mother. Both he and the daughter assumed that would be better.

> It was a tough decision for me to let her go back this last time. Very tough decision. But she wanted it, my daughter wanted to go back. You know, she's at that age—she's eleven years old and at that age that she's starting to develop her own personality, going through puberty. We began to have issues, and I

think she felt that if she was with her mom, things would go better. But I got a call from her two days ago, and she's crying because now, you know, she's getting into it with her mom.

Conclusion

Relative to other studies and census statistics on single fathers, these fathers are unusual in the high proportion of custodial girls. However, this situation provided the opportunity to delve more deeply into a comparison of father-son and father-daughter interactions, focusing on the perspective of the father.

Ultimately, in practice, the fathers' parenting of daughters and sons did not appear substantially different. The divergence was most salient in how they *felt* about their parenting. Fathers perceived themselves as falling short on a number of counts with their daughters. A few were unsure as to whether they had it in themselves to be as nurturing as a woman (see also Green's (n.d.) study on black single fathers). Some felt guilty that they were unable to provide their daughters with the mother figure they assumed necessary. Fathers feared they could not relate to or be of help to their daughters when it came to menstruation, which in turn tapped into anxieties about their daughters' dating, sexual activity, and potential for early pregnancy. Several daily activities, such as shopping, playing dress up, and hair braiding, also seemed to them activities they couldn't enjoyably share with their daughters. Unfortunately, these perceived weaknesses were exacerbated by the occasional reactions they sometimes received from others who doubted a man's ability to parent a girl without a mother or who were at times suspicious of the father-daughter relationship.

Consequently, fathers of daughters perceived themselves as less close to their daughters than their sons and less satisfied with their parenting of daughters. This was reflected in their slightly higher tendency to describe themselves as frustrated or uncertain. Nevertheless, most fathers planned to forge through these anxieties and do their part to rear strong, independent adult daughters.

CHAPTER FIVE

❦

Negotiating Racial Identity
and Socialization

Conrad was born in a Caribbean country, but his family immigrated to the United States when he was about eight years old. He grew up with his mom, dad, and two sisters. He married a woman from his parents' home country and had his first child at the age of forty-two. By their tenth anniversary, his wife had had an affair and put the family thousands of dollars in debt. Moreover, she had started leaving for work before their nine- and seven-year-old daughters were awake and often returning home after they were asleep. So Conrad and his wife separated and started divorce proceedings. The mother planned to move the girls in with her and her new boyfriend, so Conrad borrowed $12,000 from his sister to pay lawyer's fees, and he went to court to secure full custody. Because the separation had occurred suddenly, he and the girls were "like gypsies," staying at various friends' homes for several months until he could find a stable residence. After his older daughter exhibited eating disorders, he entered both daughters into counseling for more than a year and stepped down early from chairing the department at his university so that he could better attend to his daughters' needs. At the time of our interview, he had had sole custody of his two daughters for eight years. Although the mother pays no child support, the girls stay with their mother every other weekend. Conrad's relationship with his ex-wife has remained distant.

Antoine's parents divorced when he was six. His mom later remarried, and Antoine lived with her and his stepfather. He said his biological father seemed distant or absent even when they were living together, and that remained the case after the divorce. Antoine married his high school sweetheart at the age of nineteen, and two to three years later they had their daughter Alicia. Antoine

and his wife, both professionals in Georgia, were planning a move to Califor-
nia when his wife was tragically killed in a car accident. After a year of single
fatherhood, Antoine decided to move his daughter to Wisconsin to be closer to
his side of the family. It's a move he somewhat regrets, but he has purchased a
home in a new development and plans to stay there until his daughter finishes
middle school. At the time of the interview, Antoine was currently employed
as the IT manager at a large technology services company, and his daughter
was a sixth grader in a local public school. We talked while sitting at the snack
bar in his modern, meticulous home, while his daughter attended an after-
school party.

African American fathers, and other parents of color, must face issues that white families can frequently avoid: most prominently, teaching their children how to live in a society where they are the numerical and cultural minority. Parents of color need to assist their children in developing competencies in navigating within a sometimes hostile environment (Miller 1999). Although children's identity and behavior are certainly conditioned by other people and institutions, parents' communications to children are pivotal in shaping children's race-related attitudes and their sense of efficacy in negotiating racial barriers and experiences (Bowman and Howard 1985; Spencer 1983). Those communications can be crucial in preparing their children to fail or succeed in future endeavors (Hughes and Chen 1999; Johnson 2001; Scott 2003).

Thornton, Chatters, Taylor, and Allen (1990) point out that racial socialization builds personal and group identity, teaches children how to cope with intergroup relations, and conveys messages about the individual's position in the social hierarchy and which options and life chances are available to him or her. Although racial socialization has the potential to hamper one's development, research indicates that most proactive racial socialization engenders a positive racial identity, facilitates the development of competence and academic achievement, and helps racial minority children handle stress and overcome negative stereotypes (McCreary, Slavin, and Berry 1996; Oyserman et al. 2003; Peters 1985; Stevenson 1994).

Socialization of any kind is often accomplished indirectly without words, but researchers can more easily measure explicit language and actions. Several studies indicate that most, but not all, minority parents proactively engage in racial socialization (Bowman and Howard 1985). In a study of African American adolescents, Sanders-Thompson (1994) found that nearly 80 percent of the respondents recalled having had race-related discussions with their parents, especially about racial barriers. Biafora et al. (1993) similarly found 73 percent of their sample of black teens reported family discussions regarding race and prejudice. Even with such measures, the actual amount of racial socialization may to some degree be a matter of perception. Parents usually report more overt discussions than do their children (Marshall 1995; Nagata and Cheng 2003).

Some studies have distinguished different types of racial socialization. Most commonly, they delineate two categories: messages regarding discrimination and those validating ethnic identity and cultural pluralism (i.e., largely positive messages about ethnic history and cultural practices). For instance, Stevenson's study of African American adolescents used the terms "reactive" and "creative" to distinguish between those two forms; Hughes (2003) employed the phrases "preparation for bias" and "cultural socialization" in her study of black and Latino parents; and Winkler's (2008) study of black mothers in Detroit used the terms "responsive" and "procultural." Most of the work on black parents concludes that African American parents attempt to validate ethnic identity and negate dominant cultural messages that might undermine their children's self-esteem and efficacy. Hughes and Johnson (2001) examined racial socialization processes among ninety-four African American parents of third, fourth, and fifth graders. They concluded that parents were more likely to discuss cultural socialization and pluralism but less likely to address the possibility of discrimination. Phinney and Chavira (1995) and Hughes and Chen (1997) found a similar pattern. Specifically, the latter two studies found that cautions or warnings about interactions with other racial groups, particularly whites, were reported by a minority (about 20 percent) of parents. The authors speculated that discussions about discrimination were more discomforting than discussions instilling ethnic pride, so parents refrained from initiating such discussions unless precipitated by a specific discriminatory incident. Thornton et al. (1990) concluded that only 3 percent of their parent respondents instructed children to maintain social distance from whites. When they did, it was usually precipitated by a child's report of unfair treatment by a peer.

Racial socialization also appears to vary by gender, age, and marital status (Hughes et al. 2006; Thornton et al. 1990). Mothers, older parents, and married black parents are more likely to report proactive racial socialization. With this context of prior research, we could speculate that single fathers would be less likely to explicitly racially socialize their children. One might assume that fathers do less racial socialization of children because they often are not the primary socializers and, hence, have less opportunity to do so. Or perhaps men are just less interested than mothers. So I asked these fathers what role race played in their identity as fathers, in their choice to take custody, and in the way they parent. What role, if any, did their perception of prevalent stereotypes of black men, in particular, play in these decisions? Which messages about racial identity and race relations did they desire to pass on to their children? Their answers to these questions provide us with alternative reasons as to why fathers may emphasize race less than mothers.

Personal Identity

Most individual concepts of self or identity are multifaceted and can include various ascribed characteristics, such as gender, race, ethnicity, and age, as well as social statuses or roles, such as occupation or relationship. Personal identity is also a matter of social negotiation between how one sees oneself and how others see the person. When asked how these men describe themselves to others or which identity was most important to them, most said that being a father was the main focus of their identity. They assumed that the "black" or "African American" racial label would be an attendant part of that identity, but often their narratives indicate they wanted race to play an ancillary role.

In fact, two of the fathers, older fathers, insisted that they wanted to be addressed as American, not black, not African American, in terms of their racial identity. For instance, Rubin, who had researched his family name and background, believes he has a multiracial heritage stemming from two or three generations ago; he stated,

> Ultimately I would like people to just accept who they are and accept the fact that if you've been here in America for some time, whether you are black, white, or whatever, you got some other stuff in your gene pool that you may not know about. And it's like, so what? You are a human being. See, I emphasize humanness; I emphasize Homo sapiens. I emphasize American. That's what I am: True American. In fact, my sister and I, we had a discussion about that. She just dropped by because she does that periodically, just come by and we just sit and talk. And I told her, I said, it's always, it's so amazing here in this country where it doesn't matter what you think you are. They are going to define you based on their own beliefs and parameters. I am what I am. I tell people that I'm a true American because I have in me the three main groups [African, Native American, and European] that were here early, that are American.

Rubin was in the minority in this view, but many of the fathers saw their racial identity as playing a restraining role and did not want it to be a defining feature of their identity. Billy, for instance, had ambiguous feelings about what aspects of his identity he wanted to emphasize. First, in the context of discussing why people react with surprise when they first dis-cover he's a single custodial father, he indicated that he tried to play down the race aspect. He says, "I think it's because I am a man instead of a woman. Not black, black doesn't have. . . it might have something to do with it, but I try not to look at it like that. I really believe that's it's because I'm a man and not a woman." But later when asked how he would describe himself to others, he said ". . . it really depends on what group I am in, I might even put in that I'm single and black. No, I know I would, so I would say I am a single black father, doing the best I can with what I got. That's who I am." I asked, "And why would you add black?" And he responded, "The main thing I think is that people look at me and see there's not that many single black fathers around. The only ones you hear about is the ones that don't come around."

Among these respondents, most fathers' narratives indicated they were well aware of societal perceptions about men generally, but black men particularly, not being good fathers. Many of them felt their image as men and fathers takes a beating regularly. Lanny, a school teacher, lamented, "[People] knock on us black men, like we are not going to take care of our kids."

Most of this negativity was tied to the more basic identity encapsulated in the simple demographic label "black male," a social demographic designation that paradoxically seems weighted with imagery yet starved of dimensional-ity. Lanny complains that the designation reduces him to a uni- (or at most a bi-) dimensional character.

> One of the reasons I'm doing this [interview] is because of that image out there of black males—I mean that's what people are called—"black males." I mean, there's no other part of their identity that matters, just that they are black and they're male.

Raymond, the gay adoptive father, had previously been interviewed by a news reporter on gay adoption. He recalled: "I told [the reporter] that unfor-tunately in our country you can be declared special needs adoption by simply being born a black male. Because people don't want black males. They're troublesome [he laughs]."

While most of the negativity came from society at large, a couple men complained that they get the negativity from women as well. Tracy, who worked in a social service agency with mostly female coworkers, complained, "I've worked with nothing but women. And they are always talking 'black men.' They are always putting us down, talking about us and this and that."

However, most of the fathers stated flatly that those stereotypes had no influence on their decision to become full-time single parents. For instance, Angelo said:

> I see that image out there. But I don't feel that I'm doing this to prove that image wrong. I felt I'm doing it because that's what I'm supposed to do. Parents are supposed to take care of their children. I mean, I was put in a situation where [the mother] couldn't take care of him until she got herself situated, so it was my duty to take my son. I feel I'm doing the right thing.

Although their decisions to parent had not been precipitated by the desire to counteract stereotypes, several said, as did Lanny above, that their decision to participate in this study had been motivated by a hope that their stories would inform the public better about black men. Tracy, who has custody of the older of his two sons, said,

> I want people to know first of all that all black men do not abandon their children, not just have kids and just leave them. . . . I would want students, or whoever is doing research on this or whoever, to have an open mind about how they perceive black men. You know what I'm saying? Because all of us are not people who are just out there sleeping with people and having kids. My son is nine years old. I didn't have another child until nine years later.

Likewise, Dominic said he wanted people to "know that we are here and we care; not all black fathers give up on their children." Nor apparently on other men's children, because, as mentioned earlier, Dominic is rearing another man's child as well.

Several fathers recognized that these negative stereotypes sometimes had ironic consequences for them. They often received kudos from families, friends, and even strangers for being single parents because their parenting seemed to run counter to society's expectations. The public reaction Antoine received was typical of many of the fathers:

> I think part of [people's positive reaction] is a man thing, that you don't know too many men that is taking care of their kids. And the whole black thing, . . . well, I don't know what the statistics are, but you have a lot of single-parent homes. And you have a lot of black males that say "well, I'm out of here" and "catch me if you can." Well, I'm sure it has happened in other races as well, but you know you have family, friends, and coworkers and a lot of them [when they hear I'm single parenting] are like "wow really?"

The pleasure they received from these praises was often tempered by the men's sense that these were backhanded compliments that, perhaps unintentionally, reminded the fathers of the negative stereotypes of irresponsible fathering. Hence, despite the kudos, more pervasive in the fathers' narratives was a sense of "identity fatigue," a weariness derived from being defined, particularly in negative terms, solely by their race and gender. Often the way they talked about race and identity work suggested they desired extrication from its constraint, to be free from having to think about it all the time, to avoid making it their primary identity. They want to be so much more than "black males."

Children's Identity

Consequently, several fathers downplayed race in general for themselves and their children, and the black male identity specifically for themselves and for their sons. Their narratives suggest they don't spend a substantial amount of time discussing race in general or overtly developing their children's *racial* identity. However, the negotiation of racial identity became explicit when, in a few cases, a child was multiracial or not of the same race as the family. For instance, as mentioned previously, Dominic had been married to a white woman, who had an affair with a white man during their marriage. That affair resulted in a pregnancy and the birth of a daughter, Jiji, who was five years old at the time of the interview. Dominic has reared Jiji as his own. He describes her racial location in their family.

> I don't think race actually comes into the equation a lot of the time. And it's funny, because Jiji thinks she black. She is; [in her behavior] she's blacker than I am. She's got more soul than I do. And it's pretty much my fault, because I taught her to sing rap when she was two. I didn't know that was going to happen [he's laughing]. We never really talk about race. Jiji's friends are a little "ghetto," rough around the edges, and she's always saying "I am black." And I don't have the heart to say "Honey, no you're not." I always say, "Sure you are." She's even got the head [movement] thing.

On the other hand, Lanny's daughter's mother was Hispanic. Lanny explains how he negotiated his daughter's racial identity.

> [Emily's] mother is Puerto Rican. I have told her that, you know—because— it's been a couple years ago that she asked me, "what do I check?" It was a couple of years ago. And I told her, I said, "Check black or African American. If it says black, you check black." I think now they've got like black Hispanic. I think they do on some things. I said, "Your mother is Puerto Rican, but," I said, "if a black person has a child with any other race, Puerto Rican, white, Mexican, no matter what, black is the dominant gene. So you

mark black." And it's funny, because if you see Emily, you wouldn't even know her mom is Puerto Rican.

These two fathers chose very different strategies to deal with multiracial issues, thus illustrating that racial identity is more a social construction than a biological given. The first father allows his daughter to adopt an identity that would be contrary to what most of society would tell her. He also downplays the role of skin color and other physical features in racial identity and privileges cultural aspects, such as music and body language. The second father follows a more traditional strategy of classifying his biracial daughter into one racial-ethnic category. He seemed to suggest that if the black Hispanic category had been available at the time, he would have used it, but his decision to use the black category, justified by his belief that it's a dominant gene, harks back to the use of "hypodescendency." That is, for decades following slavery, many states relied on the "one-drop rule." Anytime a person had a multiracial heritage that included any black ancestry, she or he was defined and categorized as black or Negro.

Conrad, whose vignette starts this chapter, was concerned about another racial identity issue. He parents two teen daughters, and one of his daughters is darker than the other. The darker-skinned daughter has made comments indicating that people might be better if they're lighter or "fairer" complexioned. Conrad feels his ex-wife contributes to his daughter's insecurity by making comments to the effect that the daughter's darker skin requires that she wear certain colors or that she should get contact lenses to help boost her self-esteem. Conrad, too, is concerned about his daughter's self-esteem and tries to challenge the statements made by his daughter and ex-wife. He says, "If you understand anything about race and identity, you can get ten pairs of contact lenses, but that's not going to make you feel better about yourself."

While each of these fathers approached his daughter's racial identity differently, their strategies were nevertheless generally positive and, in the first case, even lighthearted. But the narrative mood changed when fathers switched to discussing their own or their sons' identities. Fathers' narratives regarding their sons' racial identities are decidedly filled with more anxiety. For instance, Rubin, just quoted above, warns his son that his identity will be somewhat of a battleground:

Yeah. I tell [my son] that because of the way people perceive skin color and everything like that, I said, "you will be categorized as a black male, and all the

. . . whatevers . . . gonna come down on you," I said, "but always never forget about the whole idea that you are still a human being and you don't let other people define you. You define yourself. And if they want to call you this and that and the other, just look down and feel sorry for them. Not so much down, but look at them and feel sorry for them.

Similarly, Raymond, the adoptive father, reflects the concern mentioned earlier by Lanny that the "black male" identity is unidimensional and constraining. He wants his son to have a more multifaceted sense of self that doesn't impose limitations upon him. He said,

> [Race] never has been an issue, as far as—I don't want it to be an issue for Tommy. He's black. We know that. I don't want that to be his sole identity. I don't want when he thinks of who he is that the first thing, and the foremost thing, that comes to his mind is, "I'm black." I want it to be something else. I just don't want it to be his color. I don't want him to simply be pigeonholed—"you're a black male; therefore you should think this way. You're a black male, so you should not hang out with this group."

Underlying the desire to downplay race is the hope that if one doesn't acknowledge or talk about race, it will be absent, or at least it won't play a defining role in one's identity and interpretation of the world. Raymond's young son sees skin color, but the colors are not yet associated with social meaning, positive or negative. Raymond hopes that he can prolong that stage of racial identity development. He says,

> Well, the thing is, I think you can dwell on an issue that doesn't have to be there. You know, he is aware that he is black, or as he would say, he is brown. [Raymond laughs.] But he doesn't see this as something that makes him different. That's just another color. He still thinks of himself as a little boy who's brown. He hasn't turned this into a stereotype. And I don't want to do that for him.

Calvin, the lobbyist who had custody of a preteen daughter, had not yet had an explicit conversation about the role race may play in her life. However, he suggested that if he had a son, he would have had a conversation with him because of the negative imagery associated with "black male." He said, "If I had a boy it would probably be different. Because my mother had a conversation with me about what it means to be a black man, and I'm sure I'm going to have that conversation whenever I have a son." I asked for an example: "What would you say that would be different from what you would say to your daughter?" And Calvin elaborated:

> Just talk to him about how he is going to be viewed. You know, I think black men are viewed as threats; I don't think black women are viewed as threats. I think society is more accepting of a black woman's success, I think, in the corporate world, and I have never really worked per se in a corporate world, mostly in the nonprofit arena, but you know, I'm a keen observer, and I have moved around in a lot of different professional circles, and I think people are more intimidated by a black man and more accepting of a black woman. So that's what I think the conversation is going to be with my son, "whether you get an education or you're a thug, you know, you are going to have to deal with this perception of who you are and, you know, there is a lot of fear that goes along with it, with who you are, and how to navigate that, how to understand it. Things are going to be different and you'll probably be treated differently in a lot of different respects."

I inquired for clarity: "Do you mean you would advise him to be more cautious or not to do certain things?"

> No, no definitely not. I'm going to tell him to go after, and not to be intimidated and to learn, and I'll teach him how to deal with it. But as a black man I find myself oftentimes trying to put people at ease when I walk into a situation, and that's on my mind, and . . . I don't know . . . I can't speak for other people, but oftentimes, particularly in a professional situation, I'm walking into a situation and one of the first things I'm thinking is "how do I put this person at ease and make them comfortable with it?" I have to do it because the nature of the work that I'm in is all about relationships, so I find myself doing that a lot.

Although many black women frequently feel that they are doubly burdened or "othered" by having two subordinate social statuses—black and female, these black fathers felt being male did not benefit them in expected ways. Instead, in their eyes, the cultural association of black men with irresponsibility, aggression, or criminal activity put them at a greater disadvantage than black women in social relations. These fathers desired, especially for their sons, to move beyond the limitations of these stereotypes; sometimes they hoped that by de-emphasizing the label "black male" they could circumvent the effect of those stereotypes altogether.

Messages about Interracial Relations

The fathers' reticence to make race a central feature of their lives was also reflected in decisions to avoid overtly talking or teaching about racial difference or interracial relations until the necessity arises. Lanny's attitude was typical:

> I try not to note . . . black or white, because I just want her to know; I think parents make mistakes when they do that because, you know, you can tell a child a black person is better than a white person, or a white person . . . you know. And I just try not to even refer to race. People be people, no matter if a person is black or white, if they are good, they are good.

James, the bus driver with custody of his two teen-aged girls, suggested that teaching explicitly about interracial interaction might induce prejudice and division.

> Well, you know, I don't want to teach them about interracial interaction. We're all human beings; we're just different colors and different cultures. I look at life . . . to be honest with you, I'm not prejudiced in no kind of way. I don't want my kids to grow up to be prejudiced. Last year Bonnie had a white classmate, and they was very good friends. Her name was Sarah, and they used to call each other. [Now] they went to different schools, so I don't know whether or not they are still associating. But no, I don't want them to be divided. If they have Caucasian friends, it's fine with me. It's okay with me. I'm not prejudiced. I dated white ladies. I don't want to teach my kids to be racist or a bigot. If they want to have white friends, that's fine with me. Like I said, she had a friend Sarah. She was white, and they used to call each other and they was friends at school. I don't want to teach them to be racist. We're all human beings, just different colors.

For James, the concept of "race," in comparison to "color," seems more laden with negative possibilities. To acknowledge a palette of colors conveys a continuum among humans, whereas race suggests more discrete categories, often with some of those categories considered inferior. He would prefer to emphasize the commonalities.

Similarly, when asked whether he talks explicitly about interracial interaction with his daughter, Antoine said he never does, but then he proceeded to describe a conversation he had with his daughter about teacher-student interaction at her middle school. As parents often do with the topic of sex, it was common that many fathers left the topic of race alone until the child initiated it.

Yeah, I never do [talk about interracial relations]. Sometimes she'll bring it to me and she'll be like, "Why the hell they always let the black kids or won't let the black kids do things that they will let the white kids do?" And I'm like, "Well, how do you know that for certain? How are you sure that they are saying that you guys can't do it and they can? Well how do you know that for sure?" And she said, "Well, sometimes it just seems that way." So I [said], "That's cool, why does it seem that?" [She answered,] "Well, 'cause every time this [black] person asks to do something, [the teachers] say no. And when this [white] person asks to do something, the [teachers] say 'yes.'" So [then I suggest], "If this person [who is] asking to go downstairs and do something, do they have a track record of leaving the classroom and acting up, 'cause if that's the case then, of course, they are going to say no to that person. If you have a bad person leaving the classroom, the teacher knows from past experience that when they leave the class they are going to take tissue out of the bathroom and tee-pee the whole hallway or something. [Then] they are probably not going to send that person." Umm, but it's not always the black person this and the white person that. So it can't . . . you can't always look at it with blinders on the whole picture. There has to be something else or some reason or something that the person is doing in the classroom that the [teachers] may not trust the person to leave the class.

Fathers also feared that overusing a racialized interpretive lens would ultimately disable African American children by transforming them into people who see themselves as victims or as people incapable of achieving. For instance, Raymond suggested that at least in his case, race might not be the only explanation for discrimination. The interviewer asked him how he would explain a hypothetical interracial discriminatory incident. Raymond said,

I'll just tell him that in some cases it may be just because he is black. In some cases, we'll be discriminated against just because I'm gay. The black thing he is going to see. [I'd like] to explain it to him case by case, but not to explain it to him in a way where he starts to feel like a victim. I really feel like that's what we've done. We've taught our kids how to be victims. I don't want him to go through and think, "They are discriminating against me because I'm black." I want him to look at it and think, "They are discriminating against me because they have some issue that doesn't have anything to do with me. They don't understand that I have the same skills or the same feelings or whatever that anyone else does." Stop internalizing other people's prejudice. But, like I said, I really feel like people teach that to their kids, to internalize other people's issues.

Expressing the same concern was Jay, the father of two boys and one girl who are in their early twenties and late teens. He is also one of the fathers who wanted to be referred to as "American."

> So my kids know that they're black, but I never want them to try to use that as a crutch, to use that as a reason for failure, or as a reason for success. I've always tried to teach them that although you are black in color, you are an American. You can grow up and become whatever you want to become. You find out that you have Native American ancestry and identify with that, I have no problem with that. If you want to marry white, I have no problem with that. Do whatever you need to do to make yourself comfortable in life, but you are who you are.

Although Rubin recognized that differential treatment based on race remains a societal problem, he still wanted to avoid dealing with discrimination in a way that disabled his son or provided him with reasons to fail.

> I think parents in general . . . in this country there are other dynamics at play. If you are not part of the majority of the population, there's different dynamics there. But it still comes down to, as a black parent, you've got to raise your child to be independent, as a white parent you've got to raise your child to be independent. And so on and so on. You can't keep turning out all these individuals who are looking for someone to blame, looking for someone to help them out. Because, to me, that's not an independent person. One of the signs to me of an independent person is, when you make a mistake, you say "Yeah, my fault." Instead of saying, "something happened, somebody did this to me. Woe is me." That type of stuff.

However, despite the fathers' intent to downplay race except when necessary, incidents between races, usually white and black, did arise that eventually precipitated parent-child discussion or actions. Such cases usually occurred at school, and the extent to which they were race driven was not always clear. Fathers responded to these with varied strategies.

In one case, Billy's son had been suspended from a suburban public high school for participating in a "game" with several other students, most of them white. Billy described the circumstances that led him to withdraw his son from that school and send him to a private Catholic school in another nearby suburb.

He was in the wrong place at the wrong time by him being two things, the tallest kid in the crowd and, I say, because he was black. The incident was about a game the kids were playing; it was a dare. Well, there was four kids playing a dare, "I dare you to do this, I dare you to do that." Otto's dare came to pulling on a girl's pants. And . . . he pulled her pants and one thing led to another. He got suspended; the other four people playing the game didn't, and I wanted to know why. [The school] said "We needed to set an example." Wrong word, wrong thing with me. Set an example. I don't care about that anymore, what can I do to erase this from his record. [They said], "Well, only thing you can do is pull him out of school and we won't put it in his file." They never thought I would pull him out, . . . because they wanted to keep him there, but when they told me that, I was gone; that was it. Good-bye. You know, I got letters and everything to prove [my son's overall reputation]. The scouting troops people came [and asked me to] "bring him back." Nah, that was it. He's not going to be this "example." This is one thing this kid isn't going to carry with him the rest of his life and that was it. And he went on to [a new] high school and excelled. It's [a] private Catholic school. He went there and excelled and that's one reason why he's at [the University] now.

In another case, Raymond's young adopted son, having been in nine foster homes prior to the adoption, manifested behavioral problems in his predominately white elementary school. The new young kindergarten teacher was having trouble knowing how to deal with him, and it became a controversy among the parents as well. Raymond recounts the incident:

Some of the parents during the time that we were having the difficulty—and this is our society—they saw this one little black kid in the room and the conflicts with the teacher and the power struggles going on, and so they immediately jumped on the "it's probably because he's black" [wagon]. They were treating him like that because he's black and he's more difficult. And I don't think that was it [laugh]; he could have been purple. [W]e did have a parents' conference with all the parents in the classroom and the PTA officers present and the principal to talk about what was going on in the classroom and in particular what was going on with Tommy. And it was something that the principal tried to talk me out of doing it. She just thought that it was just totally wrong, that it was none of their business what was going on with Tommy. She was just very—she tried to talk me out of it, which was her job to do. Because it was unprecedented to do something like that. But I also recognized that if Tommy was going to be able to survive and to grow and flourish in this community, he was going to have to be able to communicate and to work with the other kids in the classroom, not just in the school. And if their parents didn't trust him, and also if they didn't trust me, this was not going to happen.

And so I felt like I had to do this meeting. I had to show them who I am. And who Tommy was. A lot of things that was brought up to the principal a few times was, "Well what is his home environment like?" Automatically the assumption is that if there is a problem child, there is a problem at home. And that's not always the case. And so, you know, I had to go in there and show them that Tommy's dad was an educated, well-spoken man who was doing his best to take care of his son. And I gave them his history and talked about that. And the result was a lot of supportive parents from that classroom. The parents were wanting to do more things with Tommy. Wanted their kids to do more things with Tommy. You know, one of the things I've said is that as parents we can teach our kids our values. We can teach them what we believe to be right. In school the teachers are going to teach them academics and the skills they need to survive. How to interact with other people, social skills—that's not something a parent teaches. That's not something a teacher teaches. That's something they learn from their peers. And Tommy needed to be able to interact with his peers to learn some of that, to see what was right, what's wrong, what's acceptable and not acceptable. And I brought that up. I really encouraged that. He's done a lot more with some of the kids in the class, as far as going over to their houses, or them coming over here. It's been real good. But [at the same time], the week after the meeting, an interview I had done with the media about gay adoption aired, and immediately two kids in Tommy's class were moved to another room at the request of parents.

It wasn't clear to Raymond whether parents were initially responding to his son's race or to the disruption of their child's education or, in the end, to his own sexual orientation. But unlike Billy, Raymond chose a strategy of addressing the issue in a group meeting, rather than withdraw his son from the school.

Messages about Intraracial Interaction

Fathers also felt they had to socialize their children in ways to counter constraining messages from the black community as well. These messages are frequently reflective of what sociologists refer to as "internalized racism." When stereotypes are so pervasive in a society that even the subjects of the stereotypes themselves believe them, or when the anticipation of discrimination induces self-defeating behavior, then racist beliefs and expectations have taken up residence within the person.

Kenneth feared that messages his young daughter received from the black community about the inevitability of discrimination would dissuade her from getting a good education. He complained that the dichotomous stereotypical association of education with whites and the lack of education with blacks precipitates accusations of "trying to be white" when a black person is just trying to get an education.

> I don't want her . . . to be swayed by somebody else to not try to achieve because she is black. That gets kinda to a fine line, [because] one of the biggest things that will stop a young black person from achieving is a lot of the time another black person. "What you doing? Why do you wanna go to college for? You know a white man ain't gonna give you no job anyway?" As a person trying to improve yourself or better yourself as a black person, a lot of negativity actually ends up coming from the black community because if you are trying to educate yourself, if you're trying to be well rounded, you know, expose yourself to different ideas, a culture different from what normally travels from the black community. If you're trying to carry yourself in a certain way, if you're trying to have certain things in your life or certain material things in your life that are considered outside what is normally, you know, in a black community, then you are trying to be white.

Similarly, Billy's son Otto had recently started college the year of the interview. At this predominantly white university, Otto had decided not to join a black fraternity (or any fraternity for that matter) and just to concentrate on academics. Although Otto had not spoken in great detail about what was happening, Billy had pieced together some of the situation. He speculated,

> I think Otto is going through something right now at [his university] with diversity. He's come to me, he hasn't explained everything that's happening, but [it's] a big thing with him. Because he is not joining a [black] fraternity, people are looking at him saying "Why? Do you think you're these people or whatever?" He's going through it right now. . . . I just tell [my kids] don't forget who you are. Just don't forget who you are because someday it will eventually come back to haunt you. It really will. People will say, "you think you're white."

Jay, on the other hand, was more concerned about his children's exposure to black prejudice against whites.

> So my in-laws [his deceased wife's parents] are coming here next week to celebrate my daughter's sixteenth birthday; . . . those are the most racist people I've ever met. They're more racist than any white person I've ever met, and they don't mind telling you. That was another learning curve. That's one of the reasons I moved out of New Jersey. I didn't want my kids growing up socializ-

ing with white people because you *have* to, but then behind them saying other things. I can't deal with that. I'm real. What you see is what you get, and I want my children to grow up being honest. This is who I am. I'm not holding anything back and I'm not putting on airs. I really think they've [the in-laws] come a ways, but they've come about as far as the 1950s in their thinking. My wife was like that initially when I first met her. I told her, "I can't deal with that." My best friend was black. I had known him since I was twelve, and the woman that he's in love with is white. What am I going to do, tell him that I can't associate with you because of that? So eventually [my wife] grew beyond her small . . . and that was one reason she kept saying she had to get away from there. She had to move away from her small town to some place bigger, so you can see more of the world.

Obviously, fathers found that their preferred strategy of downplaying race was at times subverted by these countervailing forces of discrimination and internalized racism. Fathers responded to these negative racialized messages with several proactive, but often divergent, approaches.

Proactive Racial Socialization

Although fathers hesitated to initiate discussion of interracial issues unless particular incidents arose, three proactive racial socialization strategies were commonly expressed among the fathers. First, a number of the fathers mentioned intentionally exposing their children to activities associated with African or African American cultures, such as enrolling the child in an African drumming class, visiting black history museums, reading about historical black figures like Benjamin Banneker, the eighteenth-century African American mathematician, or Rosa Parks, the twentieth-century civil rights activist. Second, most fathers encouraged the adoption of mainstream values, a term in the scholarly literature which refers to skills, knowledge, and experiences that would enable children to succeed in American society. Getting a good education was the most common example. Finally, most fathers attempted to teach mutual respect among humans regardless of race. While the latter two strategies would be socialization strategies that many parents, regardless of race, would adopt for their children, in the case of these African American fathers, the strategies were framed within the context of race.

Calvin's philosophy exemplifies all three of these strategies. As the father of one young daughter, he starts by reiterating what we've heard earlier, that explicit conversations about racial identity and interracial relations are scarce in his home, but then he goes on to say what he does instead.

You know, I have never sat her down and had a conversation like "this is what it means to be black, these are the kinds of things you are going to face." I have never sat her down to have that conversation. I have very much tried to instill in her a sense of her culture because I think that that is very important. You know, just by talking to her, by talking to her about historical figures, exposing her to the museum, the black historical society. I have a drum upstairs; my number one passion is music, and she listens to—well, she doesn't listen to it because she hates it—but she has been exposed to all kinds of music. I'm a big jazz fan so she can identify trumpets and different instruments. I'm just trying to give her exposure. I haven't talked to her about what it means to be black, but I have talked to her about not judging people and being open minded, period. You know, . . . she has made distinctions between black and white; I can't remember exactly in what context she said them. And when she does, I tell her people are people, and at the same time instill a sense of heritage and culture. I want her to be open-minded and not judgmental about people. But other than that, I have just talked to her about just life in general, you know, education, education, education is the most important thing. You know you have to get an education, higher education, going to college; that's not even a question. So I talked to her about those kinds of things in preparation for life.

While parents of all races frequently desire to give their children a broad experience, these African American fathers sometimes pointed out that due to persistently high levels of residential segregation and poverty, black children, in particular, may have limited chances to travel, limited exposure to cultural phenomena beyond the black community, and limited opportunities to attain what sociologists call "cultural capital"—forms of knowledge, skills, education, and experience that advantage people in society. For instance, as a child, Kenneth's dad was in the military, so their family moved around a lot, and in the course of these moves he was exposed to a variety of settings and people. In particular, he noted the variety of ethnic food he had eaten and music genres he had enjoyed. He said his family ate seafood, Chinese food, Italian food, as well as the traditional American meat-and-potatoes meal. He grew up listening to jazz, Motown, rhythm and blues, big band, classical, and marches. Although as a postal carrier Kenneth's residence currently is stable, he would like to replicate this broad ethnic cultural exposure for his daughter

because being African American, being black, I never wanted her to be a person [who has] a small universe, the stereotypical things, the basketball, hip hop, fried chicken, entertainment. I want her to have a bigger universe than that. All that is fine, but I also want her to know that there are other things in the world. I want her to be exposed to classical music, theaters, just to know there are other things out there, within reason. I want her to be able to get out and sample culture, society.

Rubin indicated that he taught Kyle about Kwanza, a winter holiday created using African traditions, but that he also taught him about Hanukkah, Christmas, and the pagan derivation of other religious holidays. He viewed this breadth of knowledge and exposure to cultural diversity as a necessity for living successfully in an increasingly diverse America.

One way a few fathers provided multicultural experiences was to intentionally expose their children to other children from socioeconomic or cultural communities of "difference." Jay purposely enrolled children in activities at a local community center where they would be exposed to families of different socioeconomic classes and lifestyles. In fact, one of the reasons he moved to the city they currently lived in was that the city had a relatively open gay and lesbian community. Although not gay himself, Jay wanted his children to be exposed to and more accepting of all "differences." He explains,

> I tried to prepare them, honestly speaking, to accept the fact that, yes, you are black. No doubt about it. Where we lived in New Jersey, it was a very mixed neighborhood. It was almost maybe 20 percent black, 50 percent white, and 30 percent other. A good mixture. The biggest change that [my kids] had to deal with moving here was understanding that some people are sexually attracted to their own sex—women to women, men to men. Because when we lived in New Jersey, I knew people that were "in the life" but they were always in the closet. They couldn't come out; they couldn't be open or honest. But here, it's very open and honest. So that for me was a good thing. When I saw that when I [visited] here for those four days, I knew I wanted them to grow up in that environment. I wanted them to see life as life really is, not to say that, "Okay, this one might have 'tendencies.'" But I wanted them to be exposed to it. I wanted them to know, "Yes, you are different from most of your friends. You're different because of where you live or because of the color of your skin or . . . ."

This broad exposure strategy had the goals of both teaching children to be accepting of people different from themselves but also instilling the desire to achieve a higher socioeconomic lifestyle. Redmond coached a number of his children's sports teams over the years, and he collaborated with a Jewish community center in his city to sponsor leagues, team uniforms, transportation, and so on. While doing so had immediate practical benefits for the team, he hoped it would have long-term benefits as well. In addition to exposing his children to another religious culture, he hoped such exposure would heighten their aspirations as well. Redmond said he wanted his children to "get out of this ghetto." He hoped that they would "come back and contribute to the community—but leave first."

> And that's why I take kids—like at the Jewish Community Center—I take kids out to see how Jewish people do things; you can go swim, play basketball with the Jewish kids; you can be on the same team as the Jewish kids. You can do the same kind of things. But at the same time, their life is so much different than yours. You know. They live in so much of a different world that stuff that's real to you is just things that they hardly think about. . . . So I let them see that you can live like this too.

Fathers were not naive about the continuing existence of racism. Although, like most parents, these black fathers encouraged some mainstream experiences and values, such as education, in order to succeed in this society, their advice was accompanied by a racialized comparison. Fathers commonly suggested that black children need to do more and/or to do it better than white children to achieve according to societal standards. Usually fathers referred to education as the area in which children needed to excel. John, the father of a three-year-old daughter, illustrates this theme.

> Being black, I want to instill in my daughter that she'll have to be twice as good at what she does, because unfortunately racism does still exist in America and as far as good things or her turning out well off, unfortunately in this society the odds are against her. [My mother] always instilled that you have to be twice as good at what you are doing. And don't let anyone, black or white, or whatever race they may be, hold you back from your dreams or your goals.

Similarly, Jay told his children:

> And when you do graduate from high school or college, it may be tougher for you to advance in the world. It is going to be impossible for you to advance unless you have a good education. So I used being black as a tool to try to make them be better. You don't have to be Jackie Robinson in whatever you go into, but you better be damn good or you're not going to make it. It's just not going to happen. Most of my friends are white. Maybe it's because of where I live or have always lived; maybe it's because there are more white people than black people. But anyway, the analogy that I've always tried to make them understand is that if the world were different, if we were in the majority, maybe I would be getting all the cream of the crop and maybe I'd be looking at you [the white interviewer] and saying, "this job ain't for you," you know, trying to keep you down. But it ain't like that. The way it is is the way it is. I've got to learn

to accept it and live that life. I've always got to try to better myself. I've always got to encourage myself.

Kenneth, father of Sara, said that though he thought race issues had improved over the past thirty to fifty years, yet in order to succeed, people of color had to stand out in a positive way.

> Well, things are different from what they were in the fifties or sixties or even the seventies, eighties. I do acknowledge that life in the United States is a lot different for blacks, or any other minority for that matter, from what it was in the past and everything. But you know, all that being said, there still are little pockets of racism. There still are stereotypes floating around. There still is prejudice. Probably to a certain extent it is true that a minority or a black person probably needs to have a little more of an edge, education-wise, motivation-wise, character-wise, and everything to achieve more than a white counterpart. Plus, it's not as big a disparity as it was in the past, but [it's still there] and for those reasons, you know, I'm really stressing the academics. I'm really stressing the extracurricular things to learn to compete, to learn how to be competitive. . . . I want her to have that competitive edge over the next person, really regardless of what race they are.

Redmond repeats a similar refrain. He tells his children that anyone of any race can be prejudiced or racist and that everyone is equal, but given the lingering social inequities, he exhorts his children to fight harder, work harder.

> To me, if you are putting another race down regardless of who is the dominant culture, if you are still putting that race down or that group of people and calling them names or whatever, to me that's racist. That's a step past prejudice, if you ask me. But—you know, I've always told my kids that everybody is the same. And being black you are going to have to fight harder and work harder, but at the same time you are as equal and gifted as anybody else.

Redmond tries to stress our common humanity—"everybody is the same"—to his children. His approach illustrates the third proactive strategy exhibited by these fathers—a message of mutual respect based on our common nature and experience. Reminiscent of Neil Diamond's popular song of the 1970s, *Done Too Soon*, Antoine delineated the specific aspects of our common humanity as he described the message he gives his middle school daughter:

> Yeah, I generally talk to [my daughter] about well, you know, I mean the world is made up of all types of people and I always tell her to respect other people as

they respect you, and I always tell her it doesn't matter what race, what racial background you are. It's like we were all put into the same . . . we all bleed red; we all have to use the bathroom the same way; we all put our clothes on the same way. Umm, so no one race is more important than the other, and she kind of understands that.

The majority of fathers strove to engender in their children a respect for all races, which they tried to teach by example and word. For instance, Rubin said,

You see, I emphasize our—first of all, by example. I never make any negative comments about any other race. You know, I'm not the type. I won't sit around saying "he's white [and] da-da-da-da-da-da." To me that's the first step. I don't care, with all parents, that's the first step in a person learning about race, from their parents and the things that they say about other races. And he doesn't hear any negative comments from that perspective. And there have been times I've even mentioned to him. I said, "I see people; we're all in the human race." And I've even told him that I wouldn't have any problem if he married someone of another culture. "Just as long as you were happy with her." I tell him that now, so that, you know, if he grows up and develops his own prejudices and everything like that, he won't get them from me. It will be something that he got from out there somewhere. But I think the first line of defense is letting him know how I feel about it.

A number of fathers emphasized the *mutuality* of respect; that is, that their respect for others should not come at the expense of their self-respect. Consequently, fathers advised their children to base that respect and their actions on how others treat them. For example, like Antoine above, Tracy and Kenneth, both fathers of young children, tell their children to treat everyone with respect but to remove themselves from those who don't treat them that way. Tracy says that

Once in a while an issue will come up where it's involved a white kid and [his son]. And the most important thing I do is I just try to make sure he treats everybody with respect. [I tell him], "If someone is not treating you with respect, then you just get away from that person. I don't care who they are or what they look like or whatever."

Kenneth says that his elementary school daughter has black and white friends with whom she plays. Sometimes her friends of one race will ask her why she plays with the other, so Kenneth tells her "that's stupid." He adds,

I teach her that anyone who respects you, anyone who treats you well, they can be your friend regardless of their race or background or ethnicity. On the other hand, anyone who treats you poorly is someone who is not your friend, regardless of their skin tone. It hasn't come up a lot. I think she has a good foundation on this. That's one area where I think she is able to make good decisions. I don't really think that that is going to be a problem for her.

Conclusion

These proactive strategies of teaching their children to respect others, broadening their cultural experience, and emphasizing education target racial inequalities at the individual level. That is, fathers did not speak of the necessity to change larger social structures or teach their children to advocate for social change. That should not be interpreted as evidence that these fathers were ignorant of lingering institutional discrimination. Indeed, several fathers volunteered examples of discrimination they themselves had encountered in business transactions or in public funding in their neighborhood schools and services. Their focus on addressing racial issues at the interpersonal level is more a reflection of my questions directed at investigating racial identity, racialized conversations in the home, and daily examples of negotiating their children's racial interaction with others.

In sum, these single African American fathers struggle to extricate themselves from the negative and restrictive cultural baggage that attends the "black male" identity in American society. They desire for themselves and their children, particularly their sons, an identity that allows them more freedom and creativity in defining who they are and aspire to be. Yet they desire to do that without negating or losing their blackness or maleness. They know that interracial interaction can be fraught with discrimination and misunderstanding, and so many hope to avoid the potential pitfalls by downplaying race and/or avoiding overt discussions about such interaction until it confronts them. Finally, they attempt to broaden their children's horizons by exposing them to a variety of people and experiences as their means permit. While recognizing hindrances to their goals, they endeavor to instill in their children ways of seeing themselves and others that enable them to live successfully and contentedly in a diverse world.

CHAPTER SIX

Is Fathering Good for Fathers?

From the time he was seven, Angelo was reared in a single-mother home with five sisters and occasionally some cousins. He saw his dad every two to three years. At the time of our interview, Angelo was a thirty-something high school graduate and factory worker in a city where factories have greatly declined in number. During our interview, he seems a little wary as we sit on the couch in his lower duplex apartment, and his thirteen-month-old son sits on the floor between us attempting to munch on the Yellow Pages. Angelo must have mopped the kitchen floor for my visit, as the chairs are still turned upside down on the kitchen table. He is not sure how I will use the information; he is concerned that his son, Angelo Jr. (AJ), may have to return to foster care again. Angelo had AJ with his girlfriend, who also had a daughter from a previous relationship. AJ's mom reared him for only about six weeks when AJ suffered a head injury. The hospital called social services to investigate, but the investigation never determined the cause of the injury. Still, social services put AJ into foster care. That was the last place Angelo wanted his son, so he initiated paternity adjudication and attended parenting classes. His son spent four months in foster care, during which time Angelo was not allowed to see him. Angelo finally secured custody, but because he works third shift, his son sleeps weeknights at Angelo's sister's house. After work Angelo returns home, sleeps a few hours and then picks up his son. Although Angelo and AJ's mother are no longer dating, AJ visits her, but she pays no child support. In fact, Angelo's mother was taking care of AJ's older half sister until a few weeks before the interview. In addition, Angelo visits and helps support an eight-year-old girl who is the daughter of one of his previous girlfriends. Although he is not related to the girl, he has been helping to parent her since she was two months old.

Redmond grew up in a two-parent household, and he is one of the few fathers who viewed his own father as nurturing. He reminisces about going to church every Sunday, deer hunting and fishing along most every Wisconsin river with his dad. He said his dad made "biscuits so light, they had to shut the door so they didn't float out." Redmond himself went on to have five children—two with one girlfriend when he was sixteen (he is the only father to have had a child while a minor), a third child with another mother, and finally the two youngest children with a third mother. Whereas he visited his three older children regularly, taking them fishing and coaching their sports' teams, it's the latter two children of whom he has custody. Their mother had become addicted to crack cocaine, and when Redmond visited the children, he noted that they were being neglected. So while he was living with a friend and working as a teaching assistant in the public school system, Redmond first took custody of his four-year-old son. A couple years later, when he inherited his grandmother's two-story inner-city home, he took custody of his five-year-old daughter. Twelve years of custody later, he had completed an educational paraprofessional certification at a local technical college, then his bachelor's degree, and finally his master's in education while working in the school system, driving a taxi, and coaching several of his children's sports teams. At the time of the interview, Redmond is in his forties, teaching full-time at a Waldorf elementary school. He was about to make the last child support payment compensating the state for the welfare assistance the first two mothers had received. The children from those relationships had finished college and were now working. Having managed to secure an interview with a very busy man, I entered his home as three of his friends sat in the living room prepared to watch a football game, and his current girlfriend cooked tacos in the kitchen. Redmond and I find an empty room to conduct the interview. His son's friend is also living with them. His daughter had recently had trouble with the law and drugs, so she was currently living in a detention center.

Most research on parenting in general, let alone on single custodial fathers, looks at the impact of parenting on the children. Comparatively speaking, very little research has looked at the consequences of parenting for men (see, for instance, Munch et al. 1997; Parke 1995; Zarit and Eggebeen 1995; Snarey 1993). The small amount of research focusing on fathering generally finds that parenting experiences are positive for men (Eggebeen and Knoester 2001). Participating in fathering behaviors increases life satisfaction and self-esteem and buffers stress (Barnett et al. 1992; Gove and Mongione 1983; Russell and Radin 1983). Fatherhood apparently engages and connects men to the world around them. Eggebeen and Knoester (2001), Eggebeen and Hogan (1990), and Snarey (1993) have found that parenting provides men with opportunities to be engaged in their communities in multiple ways. Eggebeen and Knoester (2001) concluded that men who are fathers have higher church attendance rates, are more connected to their extended families, and show greater attachment to their jobs or careers.

To obtain a glimpse into the effect their sole custodial status has had on pragmatic and emotional aspects of these fathers' lives, I explored the fathers' perceptions of single parenting's impact on their employment and income, social lives, and their life satisfaction. Generally, they reported more favorable outcomes than previous research on single custodial dads would lead one to expect.

Effects on Employment and Income

In a study of mostly white single custodial fathers, Heath and Orthner (1999) found that fewer than half the single dads reported being very successful at managing both work and family. Older fathers were much more likely than younger to force their families to adapt to their work pressures. Studies of custodial fathers conducted by Chang and Deinard (1982), Gasser and Taylor (1976), and Orthner and Lewis (1979) concluded that fathers were frustrated by the demands children placed on their employment. Their inabilities to maintain consistent, uninterrupted work schedules, to seek promotions, and to travel for business purposes were common complaints. Likewise, Katz (1979) found his sample of single custodial fathers put in fewer hours, missed work, reduced job-related travel, or switched to flextime schedules. Greif's surveys (1985 and 1990) of more than 1,000 single fathers found dads more apt to have quit or been fired from their jobs and to have experienced modifications in their job descriptions because of their child-care responsibilities. Greif also found that dads' earnings had declined, and they were not advancing. In this study, I found very few of those types of complaints.

Fathers were asked about their type of employment and their income before and after custody. Open-ended questions asked how their parenting was impacting their employment in terms of income, absenteeism, type of occupation, job switches, and so on, and what advantages and disadvantages their type of employment had for their parenting.

As noted earlier in chapter 2, all of the fathers were employed, at least part-time, when they took custody. Several of the fathers who had not resided continuously with the child since the child's birth used the nonresident period to complete college educations and/or obtain steady employment before taking custody. Hence, it appears likely that having steady employment played a pivotal role in their willingness to become full-time parents. At the time of the interview, the vast majority remained employed, sometimes more employed than before. One father was anticipating a job loss, and a couple older fathers had downgraded to part-time work. In terms of income, more of the fathers had experienced an increase in their incomes since taking custody. A substantial minority had experienced no change in their incomes. However, a few of the fathers had had custody for less than a year, so it was too early to detect any upward or downward effect on income.

Many employment and income changes were due to deliberate choices fathers made related to their parenting. Two fathers had experienced a salary reduction upon moving from higher cost-of-living cities to the Midwest, which they did in order to live in a smaller city that had lower crime rates and provided good schools. One father had quit a high-paying job in order to stay home with his three children after his wife died. He was able to do that because both he and his wife had had good jobs and had saved and invested money prior to her death. He believes he would be making about $85,000 a year if he had maintained his job, but he felt he could not have done a good job of rearing three young children on his own while working full-time. Like many stay-at-home moms, he returned to work part-time when his youngest child started kindergarten. Jay describes the variety of jobs he took to bring in some money while working around his children's schedules:

> I took a ton of odd jobs, when she [his youngest child] got old enough. I didn't work until 1995, when she started going to preschool, kindergarten. That was half a day, so I found work for half a day. That way I could drop her off in the morning. I've worked in coffee shops and worked in fast food. For me [those jobs] were just [to have] an income and have something to do to get out of the house, something to get away from cleaning house, getting away from looking at the same . . . I don't know how women do it. I don't know how they take care of three kids. I especially don't know how women all these years get up in the morning, get three kids out to school or wherever they got to go, go to work, cook, and that's their life. I don't know how they do it. I mean, I think I did a good job, but there's no way I could have, if my financial situation had been different, I don't know if I could have done it.

Billy, who had been a househusband and employed part-time when married, originally found a night-shift job to facilitate his involvement in his children's after-school activities after his wife died. He worked while they slept and slept while they were at school. He says,

> I had to make a decision if I wanted to be involved with them or just be supportive financial-wise of anything that they wanted to do, and I chose to be involved with them, with their projects, with their scouting and everything.

Therefore, I had to find the right kind of job that I could work and still be here for them. And I did. I got blessed with a job at UPS working at night, third shift. So I'd leave out the door at 10:30 PM and I would be back at 3:30, 4:30 in the morning, before they wake up. So I was blessed with that.

More commonly men added jobs. James was employed full-time as a bus driver when the mother of his two daughters died and he took custody. Since that time he has added three jobs. His income is up too, not only from the additional jobs, but also from the elimination of his child support payments. He explains,

At the time when their mother was deceased, I was paying child support, about $650 a month. You just forget about it or block it off because it comes off the payroll check, so you never miss it, after you pay it for so long. Now my take-home pay is a little nicer, plus I have two dependents, Bonnie and Sherri. We use the money wisely. When I added them on as two dependents, the dollar amount is more per week, but these two kids make sure they get their allowance each week, and more!

I was also interested in how parenting affected the fathers' functioning at their current workplace. Similar to the findings of past research, a few fathers mentioned that parenting hindered their career advancement. Darren, who had experienced pay increases and was currently making more than $50,000 a year, still feared his parenting responsibilities were taking a toll on his career. Working at a large Midwest telecommunications corporation, he said,

I feel I cannot advance like I want to because of the pressures of corporate America—to work more long hours and make constant overnight trips. Where I live now, I have no relatives to care for my children. But the advantage of my work is that I can almost always leave the office when I need to. I just have to make sure I don't abuse that privilege.

A couple fathers complained about having to miss work or overtime. Antoine, who also worked in a private firm, said that he has had to miss work due to his daughter's asthma a couple times.

Alicia was diagnosed with asthma when she was four, so every now and then a lot of times they may not understand; my immediate managers or boss may not understand if their child does not have something like that or any other sickness. It's mostly if you have your sick days for the year, and then for me I can barely get sick because when the weather changes that's usually when asthma will flare up. So I guess that bothers me from time to time; they may say "well, we need you for a particular reason or a client is visiting and you have to be here," and I in turn have to find like my mom or family member to watch my daughter for me, so in the back of my mind I should be there. But other than that I think it's mostly the same, I mostly don't bring my personal stuff to work anyways.

However, these few complaints were counterbalanced by fathers who were grateful that parenting gave them an excuse to reduce their time at the workplace. They had had to decline overtime, miss a day of work for a sick child, or bring their child to work with them, but they saw that as an advantage rather than a liability. Lanny, an elementary school teacher and father of eleven-year-old Emily, said he was grateful for an excuse not to put in evening overtime working around the school, which he does for extra money.

Others said these problems were minor because they had flexible work situations and/or understanding supervisors who supported their decision to parent full-time. A couple of the fathers can take their kids into work for an occasional few hours or a day. Antoine, an IT manager, has had to take his daughter in a few hours on the weekend when he has been called in to restore computer function. And Raymond, a manager in a state agency, says,

You know, the best work I do is when Tommy is at the office with me. And I think that the reason I do that is because I know that there are times I need him to be there, because of something that's happened at school or something like that. And I want him to be able to come into the office. And so, I get more work done when he is there because I want them to know that I am gonna get my work done if he is here, so that the next time there is another emergency, they won't have a problem with him coming. . . . But my supervisor has also adopted a child. He understands how things are going to be different when a child has been adopted, and some of the things you have to do when you have a young child. And so he has been very flexible with me."

Similarly, Theo, father of three-year-old Jacqui, explained, "I work at a community center and my boss is pretty cool. Everyone knows my situation. The director has kids. The office assistant has kids. This is a job that understands and promotes family values, whereas the big corporations might not. Here it is priority."

Calvin, a lawyer and lobbyist for the school board, also says he has been blessed with an understanding supervisor. However, Calvin and a couple other fathers hope to find work or become self-employed to gain even more flexibility and facilitate their parenting.

It's affected my current position; there's certain things that I can't do because my job requires me to be in [the capital city] quite a bit. I'm a lobbyist with the school system. And when the legislature's in session, I mean, they can go as late as two in the morning. And someone needs to be up there and so on and so forth. There's more meetings extended to the evening, and I have not been able to do that because I have to be here with my daughter. But they've been great about it because they knew going in, I was a single dad. My supervisor was aware of that so it's never been a problem. But because I want her to have the best life possible, I'm looking to, ultimately, be in a position where I'll be working for myself. I'll set my own hours and so on and so forth so that I won't have those restraints.

Likewise, Kenneth makes good money as a postal carrier, but his job and parenting conflict. Although the post office surprisingly changed his start time to an earlier hour so that he could finish in time to pick up his daughter from after-school care, he was still putting in long hours. However, like several of the fathers above, rather than viewing parenting as taking a toll on his career, he felt his employment was hindering his parenting, and he was contemplating ways to invest more time in his child and less in his job:

Yeah it is decent money. That is the only thing that keeps me there right now—the *only* thing. I have to work Saturdays and I get off when I get through delivering mail, which, depending on the volume of mail . . . I mean when it gets down to towards this time of year, in the summer and the early fall, you know with the sun not going down until you know, 7:45, 8:00, 8:15. And a lot of times, they ask you to stay out and deliver mail until that time because they are trying to cut down staff, which is great for a lot of overtime, so it's good money. But now as far as getting her back and forth to her activities and making sure that she gets fed and gets in bed at a decent time and everything . . . and actually getting to spend some time with her on a daily basis, this is just not going to work. So the thing about the working on Saturdays, especially now that she's into her activities, her little Girl Scout meetings on Saturdays, now she's starting cheerleading; the games are going to be on Saturdays. . . . There's just so much that the kids have that goes on on Saturdays, and usually Saturday mornings, and I'm going to be at work all the time during that time. It's just really made me realize how crappy my job is . . . , now I feel like I'm caught between a rock and hard place because my time and my money is all weeded out in these different directions. And I would like to go back to school so I can get myself into a field where I can go and do a regular eight-to-five or nine-to-five, Mondays-through-Friday job to free up the time. . . . I would like to be in another job where I have more time to spend with her. They are going to get more time-consuming for her. I fear that I am going to miss out on a lot of that. I want to be there for her.

Overwhelmingly, the fathers' discourse indicated that parenting had actually benefited their educational attainment and employment stability, mostly by providing motivation to work and maintain jobs they ordinarily might have quit. Raymond said,

> [Parenting] changed my attitude about my work. Before, stuff that I considered just idiotic and outrageous in an office—I would have just told them . . . you know, what they can do with their job, and I would have walked out. Now I tolerate a lot more, because I need the work. I need food for him.

Similarly, Calvin confirms that parenting has given him a new perspective on employment.

> Well it's, you know, it's definitely put me in a position of why I need to stay employed to take care of her. I mean I would be employed even if I didn't have children, but I mean knowing that I have this responsibility, I need to stay employed.

Theo has been working at a community center since before he took custody. He explains that custody motivated him to work more hours and attain more education.

> I was only a work-study student here when I took custody, and I had worked summer camps here. But after I got custody, I applied for a full-time position here and got it. It has motivated me to work harder in my job and education. Thinking back, I don't know how I did it when I first took custody. I was able to go to work, go to school and take care of her during the time that me and her mother split.

As mentioned in a vignette prefacing this chapter, Redmond, is a private elementary school teacher who has had custody of his daughter and son for about ten years. He likewise credited parenthood for the multiple improvements in his life. "I think if I hadn't had custody, I probably wouldn't have been promoted. I probably wouldn't have got my college degree. I probably wouldn't have did a whole lot of things that I did. The custody made me slow down and stop doing a lot of the foolish young people's stuff that I was doing."

Many of these fathers' reported benefits of full-time parenting—promotions, pay raises, educational gains, and other job improvements—may have occurred anyway, due to the passing of time and maturation. Most people experience an increase in job status and salaries if they stay in the work force long enough. Nevertheless, while there are some complaints here, the majority of these fathers think parenting improved their education and employment opportunities. As stated earlier, these perceptions were more positive than earlier research on single fathers, mostly white, would have led me to expect. Because black men tend to be more disadvantaged in the economic sector in terms of occupation and income, there is more room for improvement than there is for white single fathers. Parental status may work to their advantage more because it contradicts employer stereotypes of black males. Moreover, fathers who complained about work hindering their parenting were more likely those whose jobs demanded overtime or nonstandard work hours. However, many of the fathers were in professions with flexible schedules, such as teaching, or with climates more conducive to family life, such as social services. Supervisory amenability to the fathers' parental needs may reflect increasing workplace adaptations to the widespread societal-level changes in family structure that include a majority of dual-income married-couple families and an increasing number of single-parent families who need more flexibility in hours and work location.

Socializing with Friends and Dates

Parents often complain that their social life suffers with the onset of children. What is probably more accurate is that their social life changes from adult-oriented activities with other single and/or childless friends to more child-centered activities with married friends and/or friends with children. Often, their interaction with family members increases. Unlike most married parents, however, single parents must also decide whether and how to incorporate dating into their families' lives.

In particular, studies of single custodial fathers, which have focused largely on divorced men, have found that many men switched back from married friends to single friends, where they hoped they would find more support and commonalities and pose less of a threat (Bartz and Witcher 1978; Barry 1979; Smith and Smith 1981). While some studies (Greif 1990; Katz 1979) have found single fathers to have a more restricted social life, O'Brien (1987) found single fathers to have higher levels of socializing, particularly in terms of platonic female friendships, than married men.

In this study's questionnaire, fathers were asked how frequently they socialized with friends and family and whether that was more or less than before custody. They were asked if and how frequently they dated and whether they desired to marry soon. Open-ended questions focused on what changes had occurred in their social lives, how the nature of their dating was affected by custody, how their children and their dates reacted to one another, and what they saw as the benefits or disadvantages of marrying.

In the aggregate, at least 50 percent of the fathers had active social lives, indicating they socialized with their friends at least weekly. Another 30 percent said they socialized with friends two to three times a month. Of those on the low end, a couple said they had not been active socializers before custody; nevertheless, most of the fathers, even those who were currently active socializers, indicated that their current level of social activity was a drop from their precustody days. Jay, who quit his job to stay home with his three children after his wife's death fifteen years ago, said he has hardly had a social life of his own over those years. However, despite his perception that he has had no social life, he does mention that he has had one girlfriend during that time. In answering, he repeats my question:

How has *my* social life changed? I took a vacation last year. I went to the Dominican Republic, and it was the first time I had been on a vacation without my children since my wife died. Every other vacation was a family vacation, you know. My sister called me up, saying, "You really need to take some time for yourself." She's five years older than I am, and she said, "You know, you gotta find someone to go on a vacation with. All them women out there, you ought to be able to find somebody or go by yourself. Send Brie here to live with me if you need to." I didn't need to because Kay [an old girlfriend] is still living here and we're still friends, so I called her up and told her what I was going to do and she said, "Yeah you need a vacation; I'll take care of Brie." So I went for eight days. So my social life was changed a lot.

Obviously, shortages of time and child care are factors constraining single parents' social lives, but the fathers provided other reasons to account for the decline as well. Billy, a widower, said that he denied himself a social life in part because he tried to compensate for his children's loss of their mother. He felt he should spend virtually all his time with his children.

I don't have a social life. It's lessened immensely. You know, I had a guilt feeling for a long time. I wouldn't even go out to eat by myself. I felt guilty going out to eat, you know. It's just a guilt thing I had because their mother was taken away from them.

Although most of the fathers had at least one or two friends who were also fathers (though not custodial), a couple men experienced a decline in social activity because their friends felt they could no longer relate to someone who had parental responsibilities. As an adoptive father, Raymond's case is atypical in that he had the most "choice" in regard to custody than did some of the other fathers. Also, as a gay man, he did not have as many male friends with children as some of the other fathers did. He remembers,

A lot of the people who I would call my friends before Tommy dropped off af-ter Tommy arrived. I think it was they had nothing to identify with me. They didn't understand the experience of trying to get someone to go to bed by 7:30 PM. You know? Or the idea that you are stuck at home at 7:30 PM. But I tried to prepare myself for that beforehand. I realized that I wasn't going to be able to go out every night. [Before Tommy] I would go out with different friends three, four, five nights a week. Staying out late, getting up early and going to work. Guys in their twenties, that's what they do [he laughs]. So I started mak-ing myself go home, being home at 9 or at the latest 10 PM right before I had Tommy. Or I would invite people over to the house, but I wouldn't go out. I wanted to adjust myself to that idea that I had to be home.

For most of the fathers, two main reasons for a reduction or modification in socializing resonated in the interviews. First, a few of the men changed or reduced their social lives in order to present good examples to their children. They indicated that they had reduced time spent with friends who would not be good influences on their children, that they themselves had changed their own social behavior, or they changed the social setting so as not to expose their children to questionable behaviors. For example, Theo said, "Certain friends I used to hang out with at school are not really responsible. They're my age and just out on the loose, maybe working, not in school, doing what-ever. I hang out with them sometimes, but less."

Redmond, custodial father of two teenagers, said he had to change his own social behaviors,

I don't know if I'm going to say I lost friends. The ones who were real friends I didn't lose. But I do feel like I had to change my ways, you know. I mean, I was more of a social partier and more of a ladies' man and all that kind of stuff. So I had to stop doing a whole lot of things in order to try to be a decent role model for my children. . . . I had to do things that were going to work for my family, not just for me.

Dominic also limited his social life in order to be an example for his children.

[When my wife and I were together, we] used to do things together. We had friends we did things with. And we don't really associate with any of them anymore. Just don't have the time. [Plus] I can't hang out and go grab a beer because I don't want my kids thinking that's okay.

Tracy described how he had to adapt evening gatherings at his house for the sake of his son:

Last night family members came over and a lot of people came over. Train was here and his cousin Earl. I barbequed and made sure that they ate, and then I took them to Earl's for the night because I knew some people were going to start drinking. When I took this responsibility [of custody], I knew my life was going to change. So, I still see the same people, because none of my friends are into heavy drugs or anything like that. I have some that might use marijuana, but that's about it. And they would never do it in front of my child. So as long as they got the respect thing, they can come around.

A second, though less frequent, reason accounting for a reduction in socializing was due to relocation. Two fathers had moved from their home states to take different jobs, and one relocated to a military base. Those fathers indicated that their social life and support system were drastically reduced. They still needed time to establish new social networks, but also, unlike the other fathers, they lacked the proximity to extended family members who would either be part of that social life or could watch their children while the fathers maintained their social life.

Although two of the men in the study knew each other and had purposely chosen to live close to each other for support, only two other fathers knew of other men with custody of children, but they didn't make a point of socializing with them. None of the fathers were inclined to seek out other single custodial fathers for a support network. This finding was similar to earlier research on single fathers (Hanson 1988).

In terms of dating, earlier studies on single custodial fathers have had mixed conclusions. Greif's (1985) survey of more than 1,000 fathers found that 50 percent were dating weekly. The higher their income, the more likely they were dating. However, Greif's (1990) follow-up found that the fathers were dating less and enjoying their social life less. Similarly, Chang and Deinard (1982) and Katz (1979) said the general themes of their respondents were loneliness, lack of a social life, and restricted dating.

In this study, most of the men were dating irregularly. Two or three were not dating at all. Of the few who were dating with some regularity, one was dating monthly, another was dating once or twice a week, and one was almost daily. Eighty percent said they were not in a serious relationship, but 60 percent said they would like to marry soon. Though a few had cohabited with a girlfriend for a short time during the custody period, at the time of the interviews, only one was living with a girlfriend.

As with their experience socializing with friends, most fathers said they found dating more difficult than they had before. Two main reasons topped the list: They had changed their mind about the type of woman they wanted to date or they wanted to protect their children. A couple of the fathers admitted that before they had children or custody of children, they would not have been interested in dating women with children. But now that they themselves had children, they needed women who understood that their children were a priority in their lives. Darren's experience led him to believe that "women without kids don't understand what it is like to be a parent, and women with grown kids have forgotten." Calvin elaborated on this:

> It really changed in terms of dating, the kind of people that I would, you know, choose to date. I've dated women that have had children of their own, which if I didn't have children, I don't know if I would have done that. And it was great because they understood, you know, they understood the dynamic. They were more accepting and I was more accepted. But had I not had kids, I don't know if I would have been with women who do. And there have been some women who didn't, you know. I would run into situations where the women have said, "No you have a child, I won't date you." So it's had an impact. Any woman that I've seen, particularly that if it's gotten serious, they have to understand that this is a priority, this is *the* priority, and they have to be accepting of that.

Lanny, Emily's dad, hopes to seek custody of his son also. He added that not only would he like to date someone with children but also someone who doesn't want more children.

> I might be sounding selfish, but I'm hoping to find a woman who doesn't want any more kids. Because we can't afford it, unless she's going to make $100,000. I don't want to bring no child where we've got to struggle and suffer. You know, I don't want the child to have to go through that. . . . I mean, if she already has one or two kids, I would hope we could sit down and talk: Let's raise these together, as husband, wife and family. It's nice to share a child together, but we don't need another one. I've never been married, never been engaged, or nothing like that. I want it to be a one-time sort of deal. I don't want to go through divorce, all that kind of stuff.

A couple men joked that their parental status was a useful pickup line—Dominic attests: "Women think it's the best thing since sliced bread. Talk about wanting to get a date, ha! It's a perfect date line. It's like 'Wow, you're responsible. And you're not afraid of commitment. I like that!'" But the men's more frequent refrain suggested that it was hard to find women who were accepting of their parental status and their commitment to their children. Jay explained:

> I have not been able to engage in a relationship seriously so that it lasted a year. I go into relationships with this big sign that says, "I'm married to my kids, and I'm not even going to consider getting married until my daughter turns eighteen." And usually what that does . . . it defines real quick what I'm all about. So there's no ifs, ands, or buts. "How come you can't come out and party? How come you can't do this or spend more time with me?" Because I'm married to my kids. I know that's a terrible thing to say, but I am. But that's the way it has to be.

Even Raymond, the gay father, said

> Just to go see a movie, it's hard getting a date. There are a lot of gay men around here who say, "Oh, I'd love to have children some day. That would just be wonderful." But when it comes to face the reality and the commitment issue, they can't deal with it. I tell people right up front that I have a son; if they don't want to be involved with that part of my life, then they really don't want to be involved here, so why hide it?

The other common reason for dating difficulty was the desire to protect their children from various emotional situations. Some fathers wanted to shield their children, especially daughters, from emotional attachments that may ultimately end. One father had said his daughter had manifested jealousy of the time he spent with a date. Others were more concerned to limit their child's knowledge of or exposure to their father's sexual life. For instance, Theo learned the hard way that his young daughter could easily become attached to his girlfriends. His daughter, Jacqui, had begun to call one of his girlfriends "mom," but then Theo and his girlfriend broke up, and Jacqui took it hard, so now he doesn't bring his girlfriends home. Antoine said that he had developed a policy of waiting about half a year to test whether the relationship was worth exposing his daughter to. At the time of the interview, Antoine was dating a woman whom he had finally introduced to his daughter.

> [My current relationship is] working pretty good actually. [My daughter] actually likes her, so it was really weird because for a while, I would never bring anyone around her unless I knew for sure that they were, you know, a good fit,

and as long the women understood it's a package deal. It's me and my daughter. And in the five years, maybe I've had two relationships. This would be my second. . . . But before generally I would wait a good five or six months before I introduce anyone to her. And that's just for her protection's sake.

Calvin suggested that perhaps from jealousy or fear that she would lose her dad's affection to another, his daughter had interrogated him about his dates. Hence, he switched to a more discreet dating style.

[My daughter] had a problem sometimes when I dated. She didn't like when I would go out; she didn't like that. She always wanted to know where I was and I had a problem with that because sometimes I felt like it's not a father-daughter relationship, because she was like "where have you been?" And we were struggling with that because I would tell her that I didn't have to answer that because I'm the father.

The inability to find inexpensive privacy for intimacy posed an obstacle for some fathers as well as their older children. Jay's case illustrates:

My attitude has always been that I've never had a woman stay at my house. Now I've had female companions, but if there was no hotel money available, then it didn't happen. Fortunately, the women that I've known, a few owned their own houses or had their own apartments, so that was the agreement up front. I don't want women in my house, and that's the reason I told my sons . . . my son was seventeen, he was about to graduate and invited his girlfriend over. They went upstairs, and my daughter said, "Where they going?" [he laughs], I said, "She must be going to the bathroom." After about fifteen minutes, I called him and he came out and I said, "Your girlfriend's upstairs." He said, "Yeah, we're just watching TV." I said, "It's not what you're doing; it's the perception of what could be happening. I don't want my daughter seeing women starting to float through the house. I think she'll grow up thinking that it's a normal process to have men flowing in and out of your house. I don't want that."

Is Marriage in Their Future?

Although at least one study (South 1993) has concluded that black men are less desirous of marriage than white and Hispanic men, the majority of these fathers hoped to marry some day. Heterosexual black men who intend to marry within their racial group have a gender ratio in their favor, as black women outnumber black men beginning around the age of eighteen. Hence, finding a woman is not usually a problem, particularly if women of other races are included in the eligible pool. Many of the fathers wanted a relationship to sate their own needs for companionship and emotional security. Moreover, as indicated in chapter 4, fathers of daughters, in particular, wanted to provide a female perspective for their children. However, most were not naive to the challenges that a marriage might present.

Calvin's dating experience has already given him evidence to suggest that marriage could pose adjustment problems to his daughter.

> I would like to get married. You know, whenever, I'm open to it. I think it would help the situation in terms of providing even more stability. But I know it is going to be a challenge because, you know, over the years, Sienna has met women that I have dated. She has always struggled. Because that someone is getting the attention. So I have always had to, when I have been in a serious relationship, and I was in a serious relationship at one point, I was in a couple of serious relationships actually. It was frustrating. It was a challenge because she is used to getting all of my attention and now she is sharing that attention with the person I'm with, as well as if they have children, you know. So you know I have been through that and I know that it will be a challenge any time you try and bring new people together . . . just managing the relationships.

Kenneth also noted the pros and cons of marriage,

> There would be someone to help out with the child care issues and, you know, transportation issues. There would be that female role model person actually in the home. My daughter would actually have the opportunity to see what a normal loving relationship between spouses actually is like on a day-to-day basis. The downside is there would be more adjustment. I think we're just getting into a period where I really consider things normal. If we brought a third party in the house, another female into the house, I'm sure there would be some adjustment, no matter how ideal this person might be, no matter, you know, how great her attitude was toward Sara and everything, there would be some adjustment.

Consequently, when I recontacted as many of the fathers as I could find a year or so after their interviews, only one of the fathers actually had married since the interview. He was in the highest income category, and ironically, he was one of the few who had originally said he didn't hope to marry soon.

Perceptions of Life Satisfaction

Lastly, as mentioned in earlier chapters, fathers were given a list of twelve adjectives and were asked to pick three that describe how they feel much of the time. The twelve adjectives were: isolated, misunderstood, incompetent, competent, uncertain, frustrated, happy, discriminated against, rewarded, satisfied, supported, and lonely. The qualitative questions asked them to explain why they picked those adjectives. In addition, they were also asked several questions that addressed how fatherhood contributed to their identity, what kind of reactions or feedback they received from other people, and how parenting had changed them.

In regard to their perception of themselves, fathers had generally positive regard for themselves and their situation. Despite the fact that the list of adjectives was skewed to the negative, the vast majority of fathers chose mostly positive adjectives. The three most commonly chosen adjectives were "happy," "rewarded," and "competent." The negative adjectives that each garnered a few votes were "frustrated," "uncertain," "misunderstood," and "discriminated against." As mentioned in chapter 4, negative adjectives were more likely chosen by fathers of daughters.

Nevertheless, the overall assessment of the effect of parenting on their lives was strikingly positive. Every single father thought that parenting had made him a better person or made his life better. Some fathers pointed to very practical improvements, such as Raymond's learning to wash dishes on a daily basis instead of leaving them dirty for weeks and buying new ones! James said having his daughters had "filled a void" in his life, and Kenneth echoed that caring for his daughter had made his "life so much fuller." Calvin says he tells his friends who are considering seeking custody of their children, "It'll change your life completely, in good ways and bad ways. But at the end, it's unlike anything that you'll ever do, and it'll grow you up."

However, most pointed to changes in character or motivation, such as being more responsible—financially and socially. Raymond, the adoptive father who worked in state government, said,

[Before I had Tommy] I had a good salary working for the governor's office, but I was always tight on money. Just always tight. Like I say, I saw my parents once every two years. The first year that I had Tommy, in that first twelve months we took six round-trip flights, both of us, in one year. And I wanted to know where the hell did the money come from? How did we do that? You know, it still blows my mind that I did six round-trip tickets, and I could only manage to get one for one person every two years before that. You know? All for the same amount of money. Also, now I think about retirement. I never thought about that before Tommy. When I've done this job for thirty years, and then make my grandkids my new job. You know, being there for Tommy [and his kids] in a way that my parents can't be there for me because of their choices.

Angelo, whose vignette prefaces this chapter, is father of one-year-old AJ. As with Raymond, parenting has also changed his spending habits. "Before I had him, I used to shop, shop, shop for things. Now I'm being more responsible, because I have to put a little money aside. Before I didn't do too much saving, because it was just me and I knew I had another check coming next week."

Other fathers indicated their children motivated and inspired them to persevere through hard times and/or to change the directions of their lives. John, a plumber, bought a house so he could have custody of three-year-old Tonya. He said,

> A lot of things changed when I became a father, especially a single parent. But it was change for the good. Because I would be doing other things that I probably shouldn't be doing if I didn't have a child. It put me in perspective. . . . I was no longer living recklessly, so to say. I was thinking more into the future. I became a whole better person from having a child and being a single father. I'm more of an understanding person and a more thoughtful person as far as thinking about others.

Redmond acknowledged that parenting his teenaged daughter has caused him to experience depression for the first time in his life due to her struggles with drugs and delinquency. Nevertheless, he confirmed John's experience.

> I don't look at parenting as having been a hindrance. I look at it as a motivational factor for me in my life, to accomplish things, to have more of a purpose in life, rather than look at it as something that's been slowing me down from reaching my own personal potential. . . . I think I got more into focus on what I had to do. . . . I mean, I feel like I've accomplished a lot. By doing it, it made me feel better about myself, as a person and as a parent.

Tracy, custodial father of Train and a new father of Tracy Jr., spent several years in a home for delinquent boys as an adolescent. He now works in a social service agency. He attests that his sons are his lifeblood.

> These two guys, they are the reason I live, you know. Because I feel without them ain't no telling what I'd be doing. There's no telling, because I mean so much stuff, so much damage has been done to me, as far as an individual goes, you know. People using you and abusing you and all that. And I just think that if it weren't for those two, I probably wouldn't even be here myself. You know, I'd probably be in jail somewhere or probably dead, you know. So—they inspire me. But I'm just hanging strong because of those guys. . . . One is my heart, and one is my lungs.

Clearly, many of the men, particularly those who were not professionals, felt their options for fulfillment had previously been limited; fatherhood had directed their lives to a new, more productive path and given them an identity they could be proud of. For some, the father identity was paramount in their lives. In fact, as indicated in chapter 5 as well, several hoped that identity would transcend other identities—such as a black male or as a worker—to which society limited them. Kenneth, a frustrated postal carrier, said "Father would be my main identity right now. That is basically who I am now. The other stuff—worker—is either a part of this role or supports this role." Similarly, Tracy exclaimed, "[Being a father], that's my whole identity. It really is. That's my whole identity. That's my water, my bread, my food, my sleep. All that is, just being a father." This renewed sense of identity was frequently confirmed by significant others in their lives who observed the parenting job the men were doing.

Reactions from Others

Much sociological theory places great importance on social interaction as the means by which individuals develop their sense of self, their identity. Charles Horton Cooley (1902) called this the "looking-glass self." That is, other people in a person's life act like a mirror through which a person views him- or herself, gaining an identity through others' perceptions of him or her, learning to see oneself as others do. Many of the fathers' positive self-assessments may have been aided by reactions they receive from others, which are largely affirmative in regard to the parenting they are doing. Most of the men reported receiving praise, commendation, and sometimes surprise or shock, from acquaintances and friends just for being a custodial parent (See a similar finding in Christoffersen's 1998 study of single Danish custodial fathers). Most of them realize that much of this is due to their rarity in society, which makes them feel exceptional. While some of them felt embarrassed by the praise or, on occasion, insulted by the shock, most were proud that others evaluated their parenting highly.

Several of the men indicated that their friends or family members had noted beneficial changes or outcomes either in the fathers or in their children. Tracy said that one of his friends told him that since he's had his sons, there's just a gleam in his eye. Rubin was proud that his sister told him that she and her husband "think you are doing a fine job with Kyle." Theo said, "Being a father is a big part of my identity. If you ask my friends about me, who I am, I think many would say 'a good dad.' And that's good to me. That tells me I'm making good choices, being a good role model for my daughter, being consistent in what I say and do, and making sure our future is stable."

For many of the fathers, feeling rewarded was intricately entwined with a sense of competency. Not that the fathers were oblivious to their own weaknesses or unable to acknowledge mistakes, but many of them were pleasantly surprised to find that they could parent and do so well. That their feeling of competency was noticed and confirmed by others in turn contributed to a feeling of efficacy. Antoine, the youngest widower, confessed that

> the most rewarding thing is, umm, knowing, well I guess, knowing that it can be done. Because people will always ask "where is your daughter?" [And I say,] "Well I have her," and everybody's like "you do?" 'cause I guess they think that I'm not going to deal with it, that she [would] go with the in laws and be one less responsibility that I have to deal with. But it's like if it is your responsibility then you should take control of that versus pawning it off on someone else and sending a check every month. So I would say for me I think it has been rewarding because I know I can take care of her and I'm going to take care of her and I do a good job at doing so. . . . And then people from outside see you doing it and say, "Okay, it can be done. Not only can it be done but you can do a great job and the child can grow up to be a respectable person and be successful as well, I guess." I would say it kind of makes me feel proud that people definitely take notice and it's like it reassures it: yeah, I did make the right decision. Even though I was going to make that decision anyway, but I was like, yeah, I did make the right decision so I'm not crazy.

Calvin also noted that parenting, having the opportunity to "create" a person, had raised his self-esteem.

> Knowing that I was in her life is what made parenting doable and bearable, knowing that as her father I was there. Notwithstanding all the struggles, I was being responsible to the situation and I was in her life for good or bad. I was in a position to raise her, to shape her, and to have influence over her life. I wanted to be her father; that's what made it worth it. And her telling me that she loves me and just hearing her call me dad and coming to me. I enjoy taking care of her, having that responsibility and being a good provider. I get a lot of self-esteem out of that.

Billy, whose children are older, said he felt rewarded by the outcomes of his children, which seemed to provide the evidence that he had done a competent job in setting a good foundation upon which his children could continue to build.

> Competent, yes. I'm satisfied with the job I have done, or am doing, and am rewarded by the things my kids are accomplishing. With Otto in college and

Amelia improving her life. And I'm confident that as long as my feet keep hitting the ground, and I am here on earth, that I will be able to continue on with what I am doing. . . . And I know that I have laid a great foundation. Spiritually, emotionally . . . not financially; they will have a little bit of a start once I'm gone, but I won't be able to take care of them like they have been taken care of. They will have to do that, but with their foundation, I just know that they will be able to do it.

Likewise, Jay's youngest child is in high school, so he is nearing the end of hands-on parenting and can feel somewhat certain that the positive feedback will be long lasting.

The reward that I feel is the satisfaction of having watched three children grow and know that whatever they have become they've become so because of my gentle touch, my timeouts, my guidance more than anything else. So I feel quite rewarded for being a father. I don't feel incompetent or lonely.

Conclusion

While it is possible that the self-selected nature of the sample may account for the fathers' positive perspectives, overall the experience of these fathers suggest that parenting likely has salutary effects for black fathers. This seems to be most true in terms of stability of employment, motivation to improve one's lifestyle and status, and a sense of competency. We can't be sure such benefits stem only or even primarily from parenting, but it is clear that the fathers perceive this as so. Identity theory suggests that men's commitment to children through fathering is a function of the salience of the father role to a man's sense of self, the satisfaction that father role enactment provides, and the perceived assessment of his performance in the father role by significant others. The findings here, then, would suggest that these fathers' parenting should nourish their sense of commitment to their children.

The most negative effect of parenting among single black full-time fathers appears to be the reduction in social activity. While their social life, particularly in terms of dating, is more restricted, their social relations with friends and family was sustained at a high enough level to not detract from the overall satisfaction for most of the fathers. A number of fathers also indicated that some of the social reduction was due to the jettisoning of less constructive activity or social circles, which may explain why the reduction did not appear to severely hamper their satisfaction.

While I would not propose that full-time single parenting be the modus operandi for all single black fathers, it is clear that for this group of men, such a role was beneficial. At the very least, fathering provided the men another venue from which to garner fulfillment and a sense of efficacy. In a few cases, according to their own accounts, parenting may have rescued them from less auspicious alternatives.

CHAPTER SEVEN

Single Custodial Fathers and Institutional Policies

Billy grew up with both parents in the nuclear family structure common in the mid-1900s, with his father the primary provider, and all the household chores divided in traditionally gendered ways. He married young and had two children before he and his wife divorced. He married again at age thirty-five and had two more children. While he admits to being a "freelancer" in his first marriage, in the second marriage, his wife was the primary provider and Billy did all the cooking, chauffeuring, and managing of the children's activities. He says he and his wife were developing a deep friendship when she died unexpectedly of an asthma attack. His two children were nine and five at the time. Because he had exhibited irresponsibility in his first marriage, many people thought he would not take custody of these children, but eleven years later, his son is attending a local university and his high school sophomore daughter was sitting in the next room watching television while I interviewed her dad. Billy was unique among the fathers in his strong spirituality and his health problems. When I entered their three-bedroom duplex apartment, his daughter directed me to the dining room where Billy, age fifty-eight, was sitting at the dining room table with a cane next to him. He was unable to stand, due to complications from diabetes, obesity, and two hip replacement surgeries. Billy's parents have been deceased for quite awhile and he doesn't live near any family members, so he is one of the few fathers who had no family support to speak of.

Theo's parents never married, although they lived together for his earliest years. Theo says his mom made a lot of bad choices and his father was rarely around and had been in and out of prison. The only father who said he looked *to neither parent as a role model for his own parenting, Theo credits extended family members and a local community center staff for helping him to make better decisions and stay out of trouble. After he had his daughter at the age of nineteen, Theo and his girlfriend broke up. He would have preferred to work out a mutual informal joint custody arrangement so that they could both see their daughter throughout the week, but the mother wouldn't speak to him. Instead, she filed for full custody. The process took one and a half years, but the court finally awarded him custody based on the mother's immature actions in court. At the time of the interview, Theo had had custody nearly two years. We talked at the local community center where he works full-time and his daughter attends day care. Now twenty-two, Theo works two additional part-time jobs and has his younger brother living with him as well.*

Bureaucratic systems, usually designed to fit the majority, find it difficult to accommodate a minority or rare case. Single custodial fathers of any race are a relatively small portion of all family households, and in absolute numbers, black single custodial fathers are even fewer. In this study, fathers' narratives confirm that institutionally and culturally, society has yet to recognize that black men can be full-time fathers—let alone succeed at it—and, in some cases, institutional processes appeared hostile to that possibility. Several policies or systems arose repeatedly in the fathers' discourse; child support enforcement, custody court proceedings, and social service access were the most common.

Most people associate the term *deadbeat* with dads. But census data indicate that custodial fathers are about half as likely as custodial mothers to be awarded child support, and until 2003 noncustodial mothers were less likely than noncustodial fathers to pay the support (Grall 2006). In this study, about 25 percent of the fathers were widowed or adoptive, so in these cases no biological mothers existed for purposes of child support. Of the remaining fathers, more than half received no child support from the mothers of their custodial children. About 25 percent received child support but often sporadically, and in 30 percent of the cases, the fathers continued to pay child support to the mothers (or to the state) even though the fathers had full custody of the children. Most of the fathers who were not receiving the ordered support felt the system treated them differently because they were men.

Dominic, who is rearing three children, one of whom is not biologically his (as mentioned earlier, this daughter was the result of an affair the mother had during their marriage), was supposed to be receiving $300 a month from his former wife, but he has rarely seen it. Whenever he has tried to work with child protective services to obtain the support or to ask for an increase, he says they are "just a complete and total joke. Of course, [they think] I'm just a leech because I get child support." Because his ex-wife is in arrears, the state has finally intercepted her taxes, but when he inquired whether the state would charge her with a felony, the agency responded that it would just give her more time to pay. Dominic reacted based on cases he has seen among his male acquaintances. "Now that's not right. Guys I have worked with, as soon as the baby's born, they're in arrears for the birth expenses of the child, and they go to the criminal justice system right away because of all these arrearages." Ironically, after Dominic and his wife separated but were not yet formally divorced, his ex-wife had a fourth child (the second by another man), and Dominic was required by the state to carry health and life insurance for that child until he could prove the child was not his. Once blood tests proved he was not the father, he requested reimbursement from the state, but it denied his request.

As mentioned above, several of the fathers continued to pay child support although they have custody of the child. There were several reasons for this. In some cases, they were still repaying the state for the welfare monies the mothers had received in the past when they had had custody. In other cases, the custody had been arranged informally with the mother, and the fathers feared that if they stopped paying, the mother would become angry and/or the court would intervene and they would lose custody of the child. In Kenneth's case, the court had awarded temporary custody to him about eleven months earlier, when his daughter's mother had been charged with neglect. The mother had had another child by another father subsequent to Kenneth's and lost custody of that child as well. In addition, the mother had recently moved in with her sister. But, Kenneth says, "they're still taking child support out of my check. . . . For whatever reason, she's still on assistance and getting child support, though she doesn't have responsibility for either one of the kids. It's taken the court forever to kill that child support order." Because another hearing to determine whether Kenneth would retain permanent custody was imminent, he was leery to push the court in regard to the child support order, fearing it would appear that he only wanted custody to save child support, which could, in turn, negatively impact the court's final decision. Meanwhile, he wishes he could use that child support money to put his daughter in a private school.

Lanny, another father who is still paying child support, admits that part of the reason he continues to pay is to prove something to the mother. When he didn't have custody, the mother used to say, "Just because you pay child support, that don't mean nothing. I got them [the kids] everyday." So now Lanny admits he's happy that he can now say, "I pay *and* I got them everyday. I do that, too. I've got one-up."

Several of the fathers had found government agencies, the court system, and social services hostile. Perhaps these systems appear hostile to most everyone who gets caught up in them, or it's possible that these fathers' cases are unusual. Or possibly their expectations were unrealistic, with the fathers naively expecting that, given the stereotypes of "absent" or "deadbeat" dads, such institutions would be facilitative of black men eager to parent their children. But instead, fathers found that these institutions seemed to drag their feet or place obstacles in their way.

Some of the incidents that fathers encountered were relatively minor. For instance, Kenneth complained that he tried to find scholarships or grants for single parents that would enable him to return to school so that he could change jobs. In the financial assistance catalogs, he found a whole section for single parents, but all the assistance was for single moms. Conrad filed his annual income tax statements designating himself as head of household and claimed his two daughters as dependents for his deductions. "For two years, the IRS refused to believe that I'm checking the right box—single head of household. They said they know I had made a mistake, so I had to get a lawyer and documentation." While these were costly and inconvenient hindrances, some institutional incidents were psychologically traumatic for both the fathers and the children.

As the reader may recall, Angelo's infant son AJ was placed in foster care after a head injury. Angelo tried to have his son placed with him but

> the worker that was handling the case gave us the runaround. First, they were saying that I wasn't adjudicated [in terms of paternity], which I was, but they were saying I wasn't adjudicated. So I couldn't even see him. So we tried to get my mother licensed for foster care, and the social worker said it would just take a couple weeks. And then the [social] worker didn't return phone calls and didn't show up in court. And we saw three or four months go by, and we don't see AJ and we don't hear from people. And this went on until we went to court and the judge said that was ridiculous that we didn't get to see him. We finally got to visit him on the last court date. But after we did see him, it was like three days later I got custody of him. So it was a long process. But when we met the foster mother, I mean, AJ was really dirty, his clothes was all spit up, and he had a bag full of clothes, and they were dirty. So it didn't seem like he was really taken care of.

Calvin's custody case took an even rockier road. Although Calvin and his girlfriend were already having relationship problems before his daughter was born, Calvin was at the hospital for her birth, unaware, however, at the time that his girlfriend had listed the father as "unknown" on the birth certificate.

Calvin ended the relationship with his girlfriend shortly after his daughter's birth, assuming that he would be able to visit her. However, his former girlfriend took out a restraining order, which prohibited his contact with her, and by default with his daughter. Calvin admits violating the restraining order several times in an attempt to see his daughter, and was finally arrested and jailed for six months. Looking back, he says he understands why the legal system jailed him because he did technically break the law (there was never any evidence of threats or violence on his part), but at the time he was shocked, and the effects were devastating.

> I had never had any problems with the police. Anything like that. And I had to drop out of school, I lost my job. And I mean, I'm in jail and it's like the twilight zone. Here I am at that time, early twenties, and I thought I was doing all the things society said, you know, take care of your child, go to school, work, and I still end up in jail. So it was a very rough time for me.

After leaving jail, he secured paternity and a court order requiring that his girlfriend allow him visitation (at first these were supervised visits that he had to pay for), but she repeatedly violated the order. Calvin continues:

> And I just felt as if it was a totally unequal situation, my coming into court as if, you know, I was under a microscope all the time. They made me fight for every little thing that I got in terms of visitation; everyone in the process seemed to be against me. The court gave me visitation, and initially [my girlfriend] just said I'm not going to comply with that, and so each time I went to pick up my daughter, she wouldn't be there, or she wouldn't come to the door. There were several times I would call the police, and they wouldn't enforce the order, which is an enforceable order. They would tell me "this is a civil matter, you need to go back to court." They wouldn't help me. They didn't want to deal with it. But after calling so many times, the police, you know, they finally took action. They didn't arrest her, but they referred [her] into the district attorney's office. But I was thinking that if the shoe had been on the other foot; if she had called the police, as a black man, I'd have been in jail. Here it is, I have a court order and they're like "well, we can't help you," even though it had been two years since I had seen my daughter.

Finally, on one of his visitations, Calvin attempted to pick up his daughter from school, but she wasn't there. The teachers informed him that she hadn't been there in a few days. His girlfriend had taken her and moved to another state. It took him seven months to locate them in South Carolina. He obtained another court order.

Even then when I show up in South Carolina, with this court order, to the police station, they don't want to do anything. I sit in the courthouse, I mean the
police station, for about eight hours waiting for some detective to finish doing
something else that he's doing. And you know, they verify that there's a war-
rant. I had narrowed the list down to five different addresses in South Carolina, so we go around and at the last one, . . . she happened to be there.
They arrested my ex-girlfriend, they arrested her mother, they placed my
daughter in a squad car, and we all go back to the police station. They tell me
that my daughter's going to have to be placed in Child Protective Services for
the weekend until they can have a hearing on my court order on Monday
morning. And I'm like, "No, I have a court order from [another state] which is
the controlling jurisdiction," and I had done research and federal law says that
you have to honor this order. They didn't want to, they didn't want to do it.
The police on duty at the time. And I told them that "Look, I'm not leaving
here without my daughter; that's the bottom line. The only way I'm leaving
here without my daughter is if you arrest me and place me in jail." It's three in
the morning, I wake the sergeant up at home, I call, get on the phone with my
attorney back here, you know, and they eventually allowed me to leave with
my daughter. But again, just the hostility every step of the way. I guess police
are not used to young African American men trying to take this kind of responsibility and they are so used to dealing with us in a different way that no
matter what the situation is, it seems to me that, due to the preconceived ideas
and notions in their head, they think they are still dealing with someone that
is potentially a criminal and that's always the attitude that I've always faced
when dealing with the courts and police officers.

Ironically, once Calvin obtained custody, the mother rarely sought contact
with the daughter. The mother also didn't pay child support. Calvin says he
"never pursued it because I just wanted my daughter. I didn't care about getting money from her or anything like that. And so all the time that I've had
[my daughter], she's never paid a dime and I've never asked for it."

In retrospect, Calvin says he had thought the system would welcome him
with open arms, "because you have a young African American man, young
male, I was working, saying I want to take care of my daughter." But that didn't
happen. He believes the only reason he was able to persist through these actions
was that he had the support of his mother and sister. He also eventually secured
the help of an attorney who was so committed to his case that he never charged
Calvin a penny and they remain friends to this day. Eventually, Calvin earned
a law degree himself, so he has since been able to negotiate the system with
more knowledge and sophistication than most men in his shoes.

Although Calvin's case is extreme in its particulars, it nevertheless conveys much of the frustration a number of men felt when they interacted with

the court or social services. Darren, who requested custody of his two daughters after a divorce, said that despite his relatively high salary (over $50,000 at the time) he thought he only got custody because his wife didn't fight it. Based on his observations of other friends' cases, he suggested,

> If my wife or her mother had contested my asking the court for custody, then it would have been much harder. I feel the system doesn't work for fathers as much as mothers. But I can't blame the system, because most of the single parents are mothers. But I definitely feel that it doesn't work for fathers. Because I know a lot of fathers that don't have their children, that take excellent care of their child or children and, you know, they are still given a lot of grief from the mother, from the courts . . . and it's kind of not fair.

In a study of custodial fathers, Hamer and Marchioro (2002) also found that many of the dads had negative experiences with local public assistance offices. Fathers said that staff thought it inappropriate for them to have children, especially girls, and suggested that grandmothers or other female kin would be more appropriate guardians. Because of those types of institutional attitudes, several fathers avoided using social services even during periods when they would have qualified. Billy, whose vignette begins this chapter, is a widower with chronic health problems. He gets by on disability payments and part-time work, but he says when he had attempted to access other forms of assistance, the staff conveyed the message that, as a man, he needs to be standing on his own feet. He speculates:

> But if I was a woman, they would be more likely to give help. The first thing they ask a woman when [she goes] to ask to get help, one of the first questions they ask is "where's the dad at?" You know, if I went there, I guarantee they wouldn't ask me where the mother was at. I could guarantee they wouldn't ask me that. But that's one of the first questions they ask, or if they go to court, first thing a woman has to do is fill out the father's name. Because the judge may not want to do something for them without knowing who the man is so they could go after him. Because they don't really expect child support or whatever [from the mother]. . . . That's supposed to come from the man in the first place.

Tracy, who is a social worker himself, elaborated on that experience from a staff person's perspective. From his experience of trying to obtain assistance for low-income men, fathers or not, he concludes:

> It's a woman's system. . . . Like I told you [in my section, my clients are] 80 percent men. We don't have nothing for them. We don't have no shelter. . . .

We have clothing shelters, all clothes for women. You know what I'm saying? All women's clothes. We have food places, food pantries and all that, but all are for women. [The men] can go, but . . . it is just a lot more difficult. . . . You have to get referred, first of all. And in order to get referred, when they call and say this is a man. The [food service] says "Well, we don't allow men up in this one. He has to go somewhere else." [There are just more] places that cater strictly to women. You know what I'm saying? They've been catering to women for so many years that they have never even thought to invite a male into it. You know what I mean? [A man can go through the system, but] he has to jump through a lot of hoops, but he can do it. Yeah, he can do it. He can get the same thing a woman can get, but it is just a lot more difficult to place him than it is to place a woman.

While this study was not designed to test the effects of one or another policy, these fathers' narratives provide insight into the relationship between institutional policies and individual choices about childbearing and rearing. They suggest reconsideration of various policy assumptions and shed light on what institutional practices hindered or facilitated their entrance into and their implementation of full-time parenting.

Policy and Programmatic Implications

In recent decades, policies designed to influence fatherhood have largely focused on unmarried and/or nonresident fathers, trying to tease, force, or manipulate fathers into, foremost, greater financial accountability; secondarily, into marriage with the mother; or, lastly, more emotional involvement with the child. Hence, we have witnessed dramatic changes in public assistance and a flood of federal and state dollars into various child support enforcement, marriage promotion, or father involvement programs (Graefe and Lichter 2007; Roy 1999). In 2006 alone, the federal budget bill provided $100 million per year for five years to fund marriage promotion efforts and $50 million for responsible fatherhood programs (Minoff, Ooms, and Roberts 2006). Such policies have been presented both as carrots and sticks and have targeted men directly or indirectly through women.

In the 1990s major changes in public assistance laws were implemented to reduce welfare use. These included lowering the benefit amount, requiring employment of single mothers, penalizing subsequent pregnancies through "family caps," prohibiting benefits to teen mothers not living with their parents, and denying access to financial assistance if single mothers fail to reveal paternity and assign the state the right to collected child support (Mills, n.d.). Such policies were intended to increase the costs of single motherhood, with the hope that women would respond by decreasing nonmarital pregnancies and accepting or initiating marriage proposals. Several studies have found some support for a correlation between such programs and nonmarital birth reduction (Sonenstein, Pleck, and Ku 1991; Case 1998; Gaylin et al. 1996) and one study found support for a similar effect on divorce (Nixon 1997). However, Plotnick et al. (2004) found these effects to be smaller among African Americans.

These policy changes were accompanied by other policies more directly targeting fathers. Most prominently, many states have diligently pursued child support payment and paternity identification. Like their counterparts above, these policies also were intended largely to reduce the state's public assistance expenditures. The public is frequently unaware that in the case of low-income mothers who receive public assistance in the form of welfare payments (formerly AFDC, recently TANF) or Medicaid, child support paid by the father through the formal collection system goes to the state to repay the assistance given to the mother. This would include payment for hospital expenses related to the birth, as well as subsequent monthly assistance payments. In other words, the mother and child may never see those child support monies. A number of states permit or have experimented with "passthroughs," that is, allowing some of the child support, often no more than $200 a month, to pass through to the mother and child.

This certainly has the potential to discourage men from voluntarily paying child support, and a couple of the fathers in this study admitted that during the period they had been the noncustodial parent, they had circumvented the state by making payments directly to the mom. In such cases, the fathers may be on record as delinquent in child support, but the mothers often receive a larger amount of money, even though the overall amount paid by the father might be smaller than it would have been if paid formally. However, in more recent years, better identification of fathers and automatic wage garnishing has become the general practice across the United States and has reduced the feasibility of such circumvention. Indeed, it has been reported that paternity establishment in the case of nonmarital births increased from 19 percent in 1979 to 52 percent by 1996 (Coley 2001; Garfinkel, Meyer, and McLanahan 1998), and that paternity establishment has a positive relationship to child support payment (Mincy, Garfinkel, and Nepomnyaschy 2005).

In addition to transferring the costs of nonmarital childrearing from the state to the parents, presumably these kinds of policies present disincentives for single men to produce costly pregnancies or in some cases for low-income married men to divorce. However, because couples are comprised of individuals whose interests don't always align, it's possible that better enforcement of child support payment, particularly if mothers get full benefit of it, might make mothers more inclined to think they don't need the father's presence, thus ironically increasing nonmarital childbirth and/or single parenting (Plotnick et al. 2004).

While punitive policies such as the above are one way to attack a social issue, they're a rather narrow strategy, given that public assistance programs represent a relatively small portion of government expenditures. Even total elimination of those costs will do little to solve national budget deficits and debt. I would suggest that policy makers broaden solutions to include policies that offer fathers incentives to parent and look beyond public assistance, as individuals' and couples' decisions about childbearing and rearing are impacted as well by labor market opportunities, prevalent wages, availability of marriageable spouses, gender relations, community support, and family support.

Moreover, recent fatherhood policies target a small portion of the population—basically unmarried, nonresident fathers whose partners are low income. Policy makers need to extend their audience to include all fathers. As this study shows, single fathers, whether resident or not, may have become fathers through nonmarital birth, divorce, widowhood, or adoption. Therefore, all fathers, perhaps men generally, should be approached as potential custodial fathers.

Evidence from this study suggests that most of these fathers took custody despite the fact that there was little financial incentive to do so. Though most of the fathers were not low income, it should also be remembered that in several cases, their elevated income was due to overemployment in the form of multiple jobs or increased overtime hours, conditions that caused concern for a couple of them and led to a heavy reliance on already strapped kin for childcare. Several fathers were also financially taxed from continuing to pay child support to the mother or to the state for past AFDC/TANF payments to the children's mothers. And most were not receiving financial support from the mother. Public policy needs to consider whether amnesty for arrearages (in other words, debt forgiveness) may be an appropriate response when fathers have custody of children. Decriminalization of nonpayment, particularly when it can be determined that it is a result of unemployment or low income, should be considered as well (Holzer, Raphael, and Stoll 2002; Mills forthcoming). A number of states allow child support arrearages to continue to accrue during the incarceration (Mincy 2002). Jailing and giving a felony record to poor fathers for nonpayment does little to help the child and hinders future employment of, and payment of child support by, the fathers.

(See also Wendell Primus's [2006] excellent discussion of suggestions for improving the child support system.)

Other than moral denunciation, policy makers have been slow to address the issue of fathers having children by multiple partners, which has implications for marriage promotion, child support, and public assistance policies. While reproduction with multiple partners occurs across racial groups, its prevalence is higher among African Americans, particularly among never-married individuals. In this study, one-third of the fathers (seven) had children by more than one mother, and at least five of the mothers had previously or subsequently had children by another father. This trend is in part due to the skewed gender ratio among African Americans. Black women begin to outnumber black men in their late teens. This male-shortage weakens the feasibility of marriage promotion policies.

Across all races, having children with multiple partners usually complicates and dilutes noncustodial fathers' incentives to fulfill child support and their ability to be involved with all their children equally. Similar to studies by Hamer (1997) and Lerman and Sorensen (2000), in only two cases here did the multiple-partnered fathers have custody of all their biological children. Usually multiple-partnered fathers had custody of their youngest children. All of the men who had more than one child but with only one mother had custody of all their children. These were always divorced men, indicating that marriage likely does play a role in limiting reproduction and obligating fathers. Moreover, some fathers may be paying child support for noncustodial children while they have custody of one or two others. New child support policies need to account for these complex parenting roles, as current policy may pit the interests of one group of children over another (Manning, Steward, and Smock 2003; Meyer, Cancian, and Cook 2005).

In addition to biological parenting, five of the fathers were social fathers; that is, they had another nonbiological child living with them, such as one of their children's friends, the father's younger sibling, or the children (by other fathers) of former girlfriends or wives. None of these fathers were receiving extra money from family, friends, or the government for these children. In addition, one father was adoptive. The potential for adoption by single men has increased (Anonymous. 1994), as most states have relaxed their criteria for adoptive parents to include single people, the foster care system bulges with children, and foster families have become scarce. Yet policy continues to abide by reductionist definitions of fathers as biological (Haney and March 2003), manifested in a focus on paternity at the expense of children. Kin care, foster care, and adoption systems need to address these malleable and complex family arrangements and responsibilities and increase the inclusion of men in these programs.

The new crop of fathering programs aimed at fatherhood responsibility and marriage promotion need not be jettisoned. It is known that marriage usually increases men's wages, household income (Lerman 2002), and access to health care coverage (Nock 2007). We also know that men who have their first child through marriage usually have all subsequent children in marriage, whereas only half of men whose first births are unmarried go on to have births within marriage, suggesting that marriage promotion policies would do better to target postponement of first births until marriage (Nock 2007) rather than marriage between unmarried low-income parents whose unions are inevitably shaky (Waller and Swisher 2006). However, policy makers and service providers must also recognize that with longer life expectancies, an increase in women's financial stability, and higher demands on and expectations for the marital relationship (among other factors), marriage is no guarantee of family stability. Parent-child relationships are often more enduring than spousal relationships. Moreover, there is already some indication that marriage promotion programs have less effect on black families than they do on white and Hispanic because nonmarital black parents are less likely to be cohabiting at the time of birth and, hence, less likely to be susceptible to marriage promotion (Wherry and Finegold 2004). In the case of multiple-partnered fathers, marriage to one of the mothers may very likely increase insecurities among other mothers and their children.

Thus, rather than encouraging marriage for the sake of marriage, these fatherhood programs should consider offering mediation programs or courses in negotiation skills aimed at helping unmarried couples and ex-spouses to parent cooperatively. The quality of the relationship between parents impacts payment of child support and involvement of the noncustodial parent as well (Hamer 1998). In this study, fathers were often asked why they thought many single, nonresident fathers didn't choose custody. One of the answers frequently proffered was that hostile relationships with the mothers presented barriers to custody. This research and others (Demo and Ganong 1994; Fox and Blanton 1995; Aldous 1996) have found that parents argue over access to visitation, child rearing practices, mothers' control over support money, and spending behavior. In this study, the widowers and adoptive father did not have this concern, but of those fathers whose children had available mothers, about two-thirds described their relationships with the mothers as distant or problematic. Another 20 percent said they were polite or cordial; only 10 percent said they were friendly. However, it is to both the fathers' and mothers' credit that in every single case where mothers were living, the children were seeing their mothers, most of the time on a regular basis. Nevertheless, surely the context for the children, as well as the fathers' anxiety that their custody could easily be ended by another argument with the mother, could be ameliorated by help from programs that provide the insight and skills to surmount their conflicted interests. Related to such conflict mediation, free or subsidized legal advice or services would help fathers more easily make their way through the complicated court system. In the case of the fathers in this study, several did use or could have used such help to get child support orders stopped, to establish paternity, or to work out visitation or custody arrangements in a more timely and less costly fashion.

The climates of social services, schools, community centers, and the like need to be more facilitative of father responsibility and inclusion. In the past, these institutions worked directly with mothers and often neglected direct contact with the fathers, perhaps assuming that they would be involved indirectly through the mother or not at all (O'Donnell 1999). Recently, many family social service agencies have recognized the need to address fathers as part of a family matrix (Reich 2005; Lerman and Ooms 1993). The use of extended kin (fathers' sisters, mothers, and aunts, primarily) for child care (which is a financial subsidy to the father but a financial cost to the child care giver) was illustrated in this study and continues to support the concept of working with the extended family whenever possible, even if they are not residing together.

On the other hand, it is often assumed that African American men have large extended families on which they can rely. But in low-income families, extended members are often taxed themselves, and the older or professional fathers in this study were less likely to be residing near extended family. Hence, a number of these fathers, particularly those who did not have access to extended family, relied on local community centers, boys and girls clubs, and preschool and after-school program to provide their children with extracurricular activities, homework help, or low-cost after-school care.

These community agencies seem to be more father supportive than social services. Green (2003) conducted more than 200 surveys of early childhood educators and found that three strategies had a significant impact on father involvement: including the father's name on the school enrollment form, sending written correspondence to fathers even if they live apart from the child, and specifically inviting them to the center to participate in educational activities. In other words, when fathers are contacted directly (rather than through the mother or forgotten altogether) as if they are expected to be responsible for and active in the child's life, they rise to the occasion. (Levine 1993 and Levine, Murphy and Wilson 1993) found that children's programs would do well to recruit and hire male coordinators to increase father involvement.

While efforts are on the rise to increase the involvement of fathers in their children's lives and education, the narratives of these fathers indicate there is still room for improvement. Fathers need to be better apprised of social and community services available to them, and access to such services needs to be facilitated. The newly reformed welfare system may in theory be designed to meet the needs of families without regard to gender or marital status, but the above narratives illustrate that in practice the system is neither welcoming nor apparently set up to easily accommodate fathers, who are expected to stand on their own two feet (Reich 2005).

Macroeconomic policies need to be addressed as well, particularly as the United States seems positioned to head into another recession. As mentioned previously, employment was present in nearly every father's case before custody was sought. Also, these fathers' income levels were above the poverty level, but as a nonrepresentative sample, their higher income levels may overstate the situation for the majority of black single custodial fathers. Unemployment is particularly high among young black men and persisted even through the 1990s' robust economy. Hence, it's not likely to improve during an impending recession. (Indeed, recent studies show that many indicators—suicide, incarceration, high school drop-out rates among them— have worsened [Eckholm 2006; Holmes and Morin 2006]). We know that unemployment contributes to lack of child support payment among noncustodial fathers generally, regardless of race. Likewise, unemployment would hardly make custody more appealing, particularly if access to social assistance and child support from the mother remain problematic. Hence, job training and increased educational opportunities for individual fathers need to be buttressed by macroeconomic policies aimed at raising the rates of employment among black Americans generally, as single mothers who make decent salaries will need neither welfare nor government-sponsored husbands. Improved educational and economic opportunities, and the ability to accumulate wealth in addition to income, will undoubtedly contribute to father custody and/or reduce the need for it through decreased fertility, postponement of child-bearing, and more stable marriages.

Finally, modifications in cultural norms and values often lag behind specific behavioral changes. The cultural messages conveyed in these institutional experiences—the assumptions that all single parents are or should be mothers, that black men are suspect parents, that men should be the main providers of their children and the mothers of their children through indirect means such as child support or marriage to the mother, and that fathering unmediated by women is virtually inconceivable—are widespread, and they continue to insinuate themselves into recent policy reforms and into institutional and individual interactions. It remains easy for the public or even family members of the children to frame fathers as either "bad" or "good" dads based on their custodial status, but it should be obvious that the so-called good fathers and bad fathers are often one and the same. Few persons fall easily into a fixed stereotypical niche of good or bad parents.

Conclusion

The normative context of fatherhood—such as what a "good father" is or whether black men are viewed as competent—can exert a powerful influence on fathers' own identities, motivations, and behaviors (Andrews et al. 2004). Therefore, findings from this study suggest that nonresident fathers, or again men generally, should be approached as if they are parenting or have the potential to do so. It is fair to assume that most men, even men who grew up without a father or who may have experienced dysfunctional parenting, desire to repair their own past parenting wounds and do well by their children, even if they currently feel they don't know how or lack the resources to do so. Few parents wish to revisit their travails upon their own children. Public views of single custodial fathers, particularly black single fathers, need to be reshaped—through educational programs or merely broader exposure through media—from stagnant stereotypes to informed visions of real fathers who nurture children as do most parents—to the best of their abilities under limited circumstances, making mistakes, and trying again.

Although black single custodial fathers have that much in common with other single custodial parents, and parents generally, the context of their parenting is more frequently shaped by an explicitly racialized experience, constrained by limited socioeconomic status, and complicated by a higher prevalence of multilayered social arrangements. Hence, their ways of talking about and doing parenting deserve more attention so that society's putative attempt to improve fathering (by transforming them into financial providers and husbands) can turn to facilitating real fathers who want to play multifaceted roles in their children's lives. Research as well needs to widen its lens from fathers who appear to not be parenting to capture those who are. The overconcentration of research on unwed and nonresidential fathers, particularly black fathers, has contributed to the impression that "black custodial father" is an oxymoron. Highlighting the choices and the diverse lived experiences of men who parent full-time may help men who don't parent see possibilities where they once didn't. Black single custodial fathers may not be the norm, but they are normal, and they ardently want people to know, as Darren simply states, "We are here and we care."

References

Aldous, J. 1996. Family time and its division. In *Family careers: Rethinking the developmental perspective*, 29–45. Thousand Oaks, CA: Sage.

Allen, W. 1981. Mom, dads, and boys: Race and sex differences in the socialization of male children. In *Black Men*, ed. L. Gary, 99–114. Beverly Hills, CA: Sage.

Allen, W. D., and W. J. Doherty. 1998. "Being there": The perception of fatherhood among a group of African American adolescent fathers. In *Resiliency in African American families*, ed. H. I. McCubbin, E. A. Thompson, A. I. Thompson, and J. A. Futrell. Thousand Oaks, California: Sage.

Ambert, A. M. 1982. Differences in children's behavior toward custodial mothers and custodial fathers. *Journal of Marriage and the Family* 44(1): 73–86.

Anderson, E. A., J. K. Kohler, and B. L. Letiecq. 2005. Predictors of depression among low-income, nonresidential fathers. *Journal of Family Issues* 26(5): 547–67.

Andrews, A. B., I. Luckey, E. Bolden, J. Whiting-Fickling, and K. A. Lind. 2004. Public perceptions about father involvement: Results of a statewide household survey. *Journal of Family Issues* 25(5): 603–33.

Atkins. E., and E. Rubin. 1976. *Part-time fathers*. New York: Vanguard Press.

Anonymous. 1994. More single black men adopting black children. *Jet*, October 31, 22.

Bachu, A. 1996. Fertility of American men. (Population Division Working Paper, No. 14). Washington, DC: U.S. Census Bureau.

Barnett, R. C., N. L. Marshall, and J. H. Pleck. 1992b. Men's multiple roles and their relationship to men's psychological distress. *Journal of Marriage and the Family* 54: 358–67.

Barras, J. R. 2000. *Whatever happened to daddy's little girl? The impact of fatherlessness on black women*. New York: Ballantine Books.

Barry, A. 1979. A research project on successful single-parent families. *American Journal of Family Therapy* 7: 65–73.

Bartz, K. W., and W. C. Witcher. 1978. When father gets custody. *Children Today* 7(5): 2–6, 35.

Baruch, G., and R. Barnett. 1986. Fathers' participation in family work and children's sex-role attitudes. *Child Development* 57: 1210–23.

Baumrind, D. 1972. An exploratory study of socialization effects on black children: Some black-white comparisons. *Child Development* 43: 261–67.

Biafora, F. A., G. J. Warheit, R. S. Zimmerman, A. G. Gil, E. Apospoi, D. Taylor, et al. 1993. Racial mistrust and deviant behaviors among ethnically diverse black adolescent boys. *Journal of Applied Social Psychology* 23: 891–910.

Bowman, P. 1993. The impact of economic marginality on African-American husbands and fathers. In *Family ethnicity*, ed. H. McAdoo, 120–37. Newbury Park, CA: Sage.

Bowman, P. J., and C. Howard. 1985. Race-related socialization, motivation, and academic achievement: A study of black youths in three-generation families. *Journal of the American Academy of Child Psychiatry* 24(2): 134–41.

Bowman, P. J., and R. Sanders. 1998. Unmarried African American fathers: A comparative lifespan analysis. *Journal of Comparative Family Studies* 29(1): 39–56.

Cancian, M., and D. R. Meyer. 1998. Who gets custody? *Demography* 35: 147–58.

Carlson, M. J., and S. S. McLanahan. 2002. Fragile families, father involvement and public policy. In *Handbook of father involvement: Multidisciplinary perspectives*, ed. Catherine Tamis-LeMonda and Natasha Cabrera, 461–88. Mahwah, NJ: Lawrence Erlbaum Associates.

Case, A. 1998. The effects of stronger child support enforcement on nonmarital fertility. In *Fathers under fire: The revolution in child support enforcement*, ed. I. Garfinkel, S. McLananhan, D. Meyer, and J. Seltzer, 191–219. New York: Russell Sage Foundation.

Chan, A. 2006. Bill Cosby: America's father. In *Black fathers: An invisible presence in America*, ed. Michael E. Connor and Joseph L. White, 125–43. Mahwah, NJ: Lawrence Erlbaum Associates.

Chang, P., and A. S. Deinard. 1982. Single-father caretakers: Demographic characteristics and adjustment processes. *American Journal of Orthopsychiatry* 52: 236–42.

Christiansen, S. L., and R. Palkovitz. 2001. Why the "good provider" role still matters: Providing as a form of paternal involvement. *Journal of Family Issues* 22(1): 84–106.

Christoffersen, M. N. 1998. Growing up with Dad: A comparison of children aged 3–5 years old living with their mothers or their fathers. *Childhood* 5(1): 41–54.

Clarke, L., E. C. Cooksey, and G. Verropoulou. 1998. Fathers and absent fathers: Sociodemographic similarities in Britain and the United States. *Demography* 35: 217–28.

Coles, R. L. 2001a. African American single full-time fathers: How are they doing? *Journal of African American Men* 6(2): 63–80.

Coles, R. L. 2001b. The parenting roles and goals of single black full-time fathers. *The Western Journal of Black Studies* 25(2): 101–16.

Coles, R. L. 2002. Black single fathers: Choosing to parent full-time. *Journal of Contemporary Ethnography* 31(4): 411–39.

Coles, R. L. 2003. Black single custodial fathers: Factors influencing the decision to parent. *Families in Society: The Journal of Contemporary Human Services* 84(2): 247–58.

Coley, R. L. 1998. Children's socialization experiences and functioning in single-mother households: The importance of fathers and other men. *Child Development* 69: 219–30.

Coley, R. L. 2001. (In)visible men: Emerging research on low-income, unmarried and minority fathers. *American Psychologist* 56(9): 743–53.

Coley, R. L., and P. L. Chase-Lansdale. 2000. The sting of disappointment: Father-daughter relationships in low-income African American families. Unpublished paper.

Coney, N. S., and W. C. Macky. 1997. Fatherhood as a deterrent against female promiscuity: A time to refurbish the Electra complex. *Mankind Quarterly* 38(1–2): 3–23.

Connor, M. E., and J. L. White, eds. 2006. *Black fathers: An invisible presence in America*. Mahwah, NJ: Lawrence Erlbaum Associates.

Cooksey, E. C., and P. H. Craig. 1998. Parenting from a distance: The effects of paternal characteristics on contact between nonresidential fathers and their children. *Demography* 35: 187–200.

Cooley, Charles Horton. 1964. *Human nature and the social order*. New York: Schocken (Orig. pub. 1902).

Danziger, S., and N. Radin. 1990. Absent does not equal uninvolved: Predictors of fathering in teen mother families. *Journal of Marriage and the Family* 52(3): 636–42.

Datcher, M. 2001. *Raising fences: A black man's love story*. New York: Riverhead Books.

Demo, D. H., and M. J. Cox. 2000. Families with young children: A review of research in the 1990s. *Journal of Marriage and the Family* 62: 876–96.

Demo, D., and L. Ganong. 1994. Divorce and families. In *Families and change: Coping with stressful events*, ed. P. McKenry and S. Price, 197–218. Thousand Oaks, CA: Sage.

DeNavas-Walt, C., and R. Cleveland. 2002. Money income in the United States: 2001. *Current Population Reports* [Electronic version]. Available from the U.S. Census Bureau at www.census.gov/prod/2002pubs/p60-218.pdf.

Doherty, W. J., E. F. Kouneski, and M. F. Erickson. 1998. Responsible fathering: An overview and conceptual framework. *Journal of Marriage and the Family* 60: 277–92.

Dominy, N. L., W. B. Johnson, and C. Koch. 2000. Perception of parental acceptance in women with binge eating disorder. *The Journal of Psychology* 134(1): 23–36.

Dowd, N. E. 1997. *In defense of single-parent families*. New York: New York University Press.

Downey, D. B. 1994. The school performance of children from single-mother and single-father families: Economic or interpersonal deprivation? *Journal of Family Issues* 15(1): 129–47.

Eckholm, Erik. 2006. Plight deepens for black men, studies warn. *New York Times*, March 20. Available online at www.nytimes.com/2006/03/20/national/20blackmen .html?ei=5070&en=05dld02ee8.

Eggebeen, D. J. 2002. The changing course of fatherhood: Men's experience with children in demographic perspective. *Journal of Family Issues* 23(4): 486–506.

Eggebeen, D. J., and D. P. Hogan. 1990. Giving between the generations in American families. *Human Nature* 1: 211–32.

Eggebeen, D. J., and C. W. Knoester. 2001. Does fatherhood matter for men? *Journal of Marriage and the Family* 63: 281–393.

Eggebeen, D. J., A. R. Snyder, and W. D. Manning. 1996. Children in single-father families in demographic perspective. *Journal of Family Issues* 17:441–65.

Eilperin, J. 2008. Obama discusses duties of fatherhood. *Washington Post* online. Available from www.washingtonpost.com/wp-dyn/content/article/2008/06/15/ AR2008061502009.html.

Erickson, E. H. 1963. *Childhood and society.* 2nd ed. New York: Norton.

Erickson, E. H. 1964. *Insight and responsibility.* New York: Norton.

Erickson, E. H. 1974. *Dimensions of a new identity.* New York: Norton.

Forste, R. 2002. Where are all the men? A conceptual analysis of the role of men in family formation. *Journal of Family Issues* 23(5): 579–600.

Fox, G. L., and P. W. Blanton. 1995. Noncustodial fathers following divorce. *Marriage & Family Review* 20(1–2): 257–82.

Fox, G. L., and C. Bruce. 2001. Conditional fatherhood: Identity theory and parental investment theory as alternative sources of explanation of fathering. *Journal of Marriage and the Family* 63(2): 394–403.

Fox, G. L., and R. F. Kelly. 1995. Determinants of child custody arrangements at divorce. *Journal of Marriage and the Family* 57: 693–708.

Furstenberg, F. F., Jr., and K. Harris. 1993. When and why fathers matter: Impacts of father involvement on the children of adolescent mothers. In *Young unwed fathers: Changing roles and emerging policies*, ed. R. Lerman and T. Ooms, 117–38. Philadelphia: Temple University Press.

Furstenberg, F. F., Jr., S. P. Morgan, and P. D. Allison. 1987. Paternal participation and children's well-being after marital dissolution. *American Sociological Review* 52: 695–701.

Furstenberg, F. F., Jr., C. W. Nord, J. L. Peterson, and N. Zill. 1983. The life course of children of divorce: Marital disruption and parental contact. *American Sociological Review* 48: 656–68.

Gaertner, B. M., T. L. Spinrad, N. Eisenberg, and K. A. Greving. 2007. Parental child-rearing attitudes as correlates of father involvement during infancy. *Journal of Marriage and Family* 69(4): 962–1004.

Garfinkel, I., S. S. McLanahan, and D. R. Meyer. 1998. A brief history of child support policies in the United States. In *Fathers under fire: The revolution in child support enforcement*, ed. I. Garfinkel, S. S. McLanahan, D. R. Meyer, and J. A. Seltzer, 117–138. New York: Russell Sage Foundation.

Gasser, R. D., and C. M. Taylor. 1976. Role adjustment of single fathers with dependent children. *Family Coordinator* 25(4): 397–401.

Gaylin, D., I. Garfinkel, S. S. McLanahan, and C. C. Huang. 1996. Will child support enforcement reduce nonmarital childbearing? Paper presented at the annual meeting of the Population Association of America.

Gennetian, L. A., and V. Knox. 2004. The effects of a Minnesota welfare reform program on marital stability six years later. *Population Research & Policy Review* 23(5–6): 567–93.

Gersick, K. E. 1979. Fathers by choice: Divorced men who receive custody of their children. In *Separation and Divorce*, ed. G. Levinger and O. Noles. New York: Basic.

Gove. W. R., and T. W. Mongione. 1983. Social roles, sex roles, and psychological distress: Additive and interactive models of sex differences. *Journal of Health and Social Behavior* 24: 300–312.

Graefe, D. R., and D. T. Lichter. 2007. When unwed mothers marry: The marital and cohabiting partners of midlife women. *Journal of Family Issues* 28(5): 595–622.

Grall, T. S. 2006. Custodial mothers and fathers and their child support: 2003. In *Current population reports*. Washington, DC: U.S. Census Bureau.

Green, C. Forthcoming. Single custodial fathers and mothers meeting the challenge: A comparative note.

Green, S. 2003. Reaching out to fathers: An examination of staff efforts that lead to greater father involvement in early childhood programs. *Early Childhood Research & Practice* 5(2): whole issue.

Greif, G. L. 1985. Children and housework in the single father family. *Family Relations* 34(3): 353–57.

Greif, G. L. 1990. *The daddy track and the single father*. Lexington, MA: Lexington Books.

Greif, G. L., and A. DeMaris. 1989. Single custodial fathers in contested custody suits. *Journal of Psychiatry and Law* 17: 223–38.

Guttman, J. 1982. The divorced father: A review of the issues and the research. *Journal of Comparative Family Studies* 20(2): 247–61.

Hamer, J. 1997. The fathers of "fatherless" black children. *Families in Society: The Journal of Contemporary Human Services* 78(6): 564–78.

Hamer, J. 1998. What African-American noncustodial fathers say inhibits and enhances their involvement with children. *Western Journal of Black Studies* 22(2): 117–27.

Hamer, J., and K. Marchioro. 2002. Becoming custodial dads: Exploring parenting among low-income and working-class African American fathers. *Journal of Marriage and Family* 64 (February): 116–29.

Haney, L., and M. March. 2003. Married fathers and caring daddies: Welfare reform and the discursive politics of paternity. *Social Problems* 50(4): 461–81.

Hanson, S. M. H. 1981. Single custodial fathers and the parent-child relationship. *Nursing Research* 30: 202–4.

Hanson, S. M. H. 1985. Single fathers with custody: A synthesis of the literature. In *The one-parent family in the 1980s: Perspectives and bibliography 1978–1984*, ed. B. Schlesinger. Toronto: University of Toronto Press.

Hanson, S. M. H. 1986. Parent-child relationships in single-father families. In *Men in Families*, ed. R. Lewis and B. Salts, 181–95. Beverly Hills, CA: Sage.

Hanson, S. M. H. 1988. Divorced fathers with custody. In *Fatherhood today: Men's changing role in the family*, ed. Phyllis Bronstein and Carolyn Pape Cowan, 166–94. New York: John Wiley & Sons.

Harris, K. M., F. F. Furstenberg Jr., and J. K. Marmer. 1998. Paternal involvement with adolescents in intact families: The influence of fathers over the life course. *Demography* 35(2): 201–16.

Harris, K. M., and S. P. Morgan. 1991. Fathers, sons, and daughters: Differential paternal involvement in parenting. *Journal of Marriage and the Family* 53: 431–44.

Haskins, R. 2006. Poor fathers and public policy: What is to be done? In *Black males left behind*, ed. R. Mincy, 249–92. Washington, DC: The Urban Institute Press.

Hatchett, B. F., K. Holmes, D. A. Duran, and C. Davis. 2000. African Americans and research participation: The recruitment process. *Journal of Black Studies* 30: 664–75.

Hawkins, A. J., S. L. Christiansen, K. P. Sargent, and E. J. Hill. 1993. Rethinking fathers' involvement in child care. *Journal of Family Issues* 14: 531–49.

Heath, D. T., and D. K. Orthner. 1999. Stress and adaptation among male and female single parents. *Journal of Family Issues* 20(4): 557–87.

Hofferth, S. 2003. Race/ethnic differences in father involvement in two-parent families: Culture, context, or economy? *Journal of Family Issues* 24(2): 185–216.

Holmes, S. A., and R. Morin. 2006. Poll reveals a contradictory portrait shaded with promise and doubt. *Washington Post* June 4, A01. Available from www.washingtonpost.com/wpdyn/content/article/2006/06/03/AR2006060300695.html.

Holzer, H., S. Raphael, and M. Stoll. 2002. How do crime and incarceration affect the employment prospects of less-educated young black men? Paper presented at Extending Opportunity Conference, Washington DC, May.

Hughes, D. 2003. Correlates of African American and Latino parents' messages to children about ethnicity and race: A comparative study of racial socialization. *American Journal of Community Psychology* 31(1–2): 15–33.

Hughes, D., and L. Chen. 1997. When and what parents tell children about race: An examination of race-related socialization among African American families. *Applied Developmental Science* 1(4): 200–214.

Hughes, D. L., and L. A. Chen. 1999. The nature of parents' race-related communications to children: A developmental perspective. In *Child psychology: A handbook of contemporary issues*, ed. L. Balter and C. S. Tamis-Lemonda, 467–90. Philadelphia: Psychology Press.

Hughes, D., and D. Johnson. 2001. Correlates in children's experiences of parents' racial socialization behaviors. *Journal of Marriage and Family* 63(4): 981–95.

Hughes, D., J. Rodriguez, E. P. Smith, D. J. Johnson, H. C. Stevenson, and P. Spicer. 2006. Parents' ethnic-racial socialization practices: A review of research and directions for future study. *Developmental Psychology* 42: 747–70.

Hunter, A. G., C. A. Friend, S. Y. Murphy, A. Rollins, M. Williams-Wheeler, and J. Laughinghouse. 2006. Loss, survival, and redemption: African American male youths' reflections on life without fathers, manhood, and coming of age. *Youth & Society* 37(4): 423–52.

Ihinger-Tallman, M., K. Pasley, and C. Buehler. 1995. Developing a middle-range theory of father involvement post divorce. In *Fatherhood: Contemporary theory, research and social policy*, ed. William Marsiglio, 57–77. Thousand Oaks, CA: Sage.

Johnson, D. J. 2001. Parental characteristics, racial stress, and racial socialization processes as predictors of racial coping in middle childhood. In *Forging links: Clinical/ developmental perspective of African American children*, ed. A. Neal-Barnett, 57–74. Westport, CT: Greenwood.

Katz, A. J. 1979. Lone fathers: Perspectives and implications for family policy. *Family Coordinator* 28(4): 521–27.

Katzev, A. R., R. L.Warner, and A. C. Acock. 1994. Girls or boys? Relationship of child gender to marital stability. *Journal of Marriage and the Family* 56(2): 89–100.

Keshet, H. F., and K. N. Rosenthal. 1976. Single-parent families: A new study. *Children Today* 7(3): 13–17.

King, A. E. O. 1999. African American males' attitudes toward marriage: An exploratory study. *Journal of African American Studies*, 4(1): 71–89.

Kotre, J. 1984. *Outliving the self: Generativity and the interpretation of lives*. Baltimore: Johns Hopkins University Press.

Leite, R. 2007. An exploration of aspects of boundary ambiguity among young, unmarried fathers during the prenatal period. *Family Relations* 56: 162–74.

Lerman, R. I. 1993. Employment patterns of unwed fathers and public policy. In *Young unwed fathers: Changing roles and emerging policies*, ed. R. I. Lerman and T. J. Ooms, 316–34. Philadelphia, PA: Temple University Press.

Lerman, R. I. 2002. *Marriage and the economic well-being of families with children: A review of the literature*. Washington, DC: Urban Institute.

Lerman, R. I., and T. J. Ooms. 1993. *Young unwed fathers: Changing roles and emerging policies*. Philadelphia: Temple University Press.

Lerman, R. I., and E. Sorensen. 2000. Father involvement with their nonmarital children: Patterns, determinants, and effects on their earnings. *Marriage and Family Review* 29(2–3): 137–58.

Levine, J. A. 1993. Involving fathers in Head Start: A framework for public policy and program development. *Families in Society* 74: 4–19.

Levine, J., D. Murphy, and S. Wilson. 1993. *Getting men involved: Strategies for early childhood programs.* New York: Scholastic, Inc.

Lewis, D. 2001. Identity, work and parenting: Implications for welfare reform. Illinois Families Study Policy Brief #2 (December): 1–4.

Lichter, D. T., D. R. Graefe, and J. B. Brown. 2003. Is marriage a panacea? Union formation among economically disadvantaged unwed mothers. *Social Problems* 50: 60–86.

Lichter, D. T., D. McLaughlin, G. Kephart, and D. Landry. 1992. Race and the retreat from marriage: A shortage of marriageable men. *American Sociological Review* 57(6): 781–99.

Manning, W. D., S. D. Steward, and P. J. Smock. 2003. The complexity of fathers' parenting responsibilities and involvement with nonresident children. *Journal of Family Issues* 24(5): 645–67.

Manning, W. D. and P. J. Smock. 1999. New families and nonresident father-child visitation. *Social Forces* 78, 87–116.

Mare, R. D., and C. Winship. 1991. Socioeconomic change and the decline of marriage for blacks and whites. In *The urban underclass,* ed. C. Jencks and P. E. Peterson, 175–95. Washington, DC: The Brookings Institution.

Marshall, S. 1995. Ethnic socialization of African American children: Implications for parenting, identity development, and academic achievement. *Journal of Youth and Adolescence* 24: 377–96.

Marsiglio, W. 1991. Paternal engagement activities with minor children. *Journal of Marriage and the Family* 53: 973–86.

Marsiglio, W., P. Amato, R. D. Day, and M. E. Lamb. 2000. Scholarship on fatherhood in the 1990s and beyond. *Journal of Marriage and the Family* 62: 1173–91.

Marsiglio, W., K. Roy, and G. L. Fox, eds. 2005. *Situated fathering: A focus on physical and social spaces.* Lanham, MD: Rowman & Littlefield.

Matthews-Armstead, E. Forthcoming. Daughters' constructions of connectedness to their non-resident fathers.

McAdoo, J. 1981. Involvement of fathers in the socialization of black children. In *Black families,* ed. H. P. McAdoo, 225–37. Newbury Park, CA: Sage.

McAdoo, J. L. 1993. The roles of African American fathers: An ecological perspective. *Families in Society: The Journal of Contemporary Human Services* 74(1): 28–35.

McCreary, M. L., L. A. Slavin, and E. J. Berry. 1996. Predicting problem behavior and self-esteem among African American adolescents. *Journal of Adolescent Research* 11(2): 216–34.

McLanahan, S., and L. Casper. 1995. Growing Diversity and Inequality in the American Family. In *State of the Union: America in the 1990s,* vol. 2, *Social Trends,* ed. Reynolds Farley, 1–45. New York: Russell Sage Foundation.

McLanahan, S., I. Garfinkel, N. E. Reichman, and J. O. Teitler. 2001. Unwed parents or fragile families? Implications for welfare and child support policy. Center for Research on Child Well-being Working Paper #00-04. Available from www.columbia.edu/cu/ssw/projects/surcent/Publications/WP00-04-FF-McLanahan.pdf.

Menning, C. I. 2002. Absent parents are more than money: The joint effect of activities and financial support on youths' educational attainment. *Journal of Family Issues* 23(5): 648–71.

Meyer, D. R., M. Cancian, and S. Cook. 2005. Multiple-partner fertility: Incidence and implications for child support policy. *Institute for Research on Poverty*. Discussion Paper no. 1300-05. www.irp.wisc.edu.

Meyer, D. R., and S. Garasky. 1993. Custodial fathers: Myths, realities, and child support policy. *Journal of Marriage and the Family* 55 (February): 73–89.

Miller, D. B. 1999. Racial socialization and racial identity: Can they promote resiliency for African American adolescents? *Adolescence* 34(135): 493–501.

Mills, C. Forthcoming. Fostering fatherhood through child support policy.

Mincy, R., ed. 2006. *Black males left behind.* Washington, DC: The Urban Institute Press.

Mincy, R. 2002. What about black fathers? *The American Prospect*, April 8, 58.

Mincy, R., I. Garfinkel, and L. Nepomnyaschy. 2005. In-hospital paternity establishment and father involvement in fragile families. *Journal of Marriage and Family* 67 (August): 611–26.

Minoff, E., T. Ooms, and P. Roberts. 2006. Healthy marriage and responsible fatherhood grants: Announcement overview. Center for Law and Social Policy. www.clasp.org.

Morgan, S. P., D. N. Lye, and G. A. Condran. 1988. Sons, daughters, and the risk of marital disruption. *American Journal of Sociology* 94: 110–29.

Mott, F. L. 1990. When is a father really gone? Paternal-child conduct in father-absent homes. *Demography* 27(4): 499–517.

Munch, A., J. M. McPherson, and I. Smith-Lovin. 1997. Gender, children, and social contact: The effects of childrearing for men and women. *American Sociological Review* 62: 509–20.

Nagata, D. K., and W. J. Y. Cheng. 2003. Intergenerational communication of race-related trauma by Japanese American former internees. *American Journal of Orthopsychiatry* 73(3): 266–78.

Nixon, L. A. 1997. The effect of child support enforcement on marital dissolution. *Journal of Human Resources* 32(1): 159–81.

Nock, S. L. 2007. Marital and unmarried births to men: Complex patterns of fatherhood: Evidence from the National Survey of Family Growth, 2002. U.S. Department of Health and Human Services, Office of the Assistant Secretary for Planning and Evaluation. Available from http://aspe.hhs.gov/hsp/07/births-to-men/rb.htm.

O'Brien, M. 1987. Patterns of kinship and friendship among lone fathers. In *Reassessing fatherhood: New observations on fathers and the modern family*, ed. M. Lewis and C. O'Brien, 225–45. London: Sage.

O'Donnell, J. M. 1999. Involvement of African American fathers in kinship foster care services. *Social Work* 44(5): 428–41.

Ohalete, N. 2007. Adolescent sexual debut: A case for studying African American father-adolescent reproductive health communication. *Journal of Black Studies* 37(5): 737–52.

Ooms, T., S. Bouchet, and M. Parke. 2004. *Beyond marriage licenses: Efforts in states to strengthen marriage and two-parent families.* Washington, DC: Center for Law and Social Policy.

Orthner, D., T. Brown, and D. Ferguson. 1976. Single-parent fatherhood: An emerging family lifestyle. *Family Coordinator* 25(4): 429–37.

Orthner, D. and K. Lewis. 1979. Evidence of single father competence in child rearing. *Family Law Quarterly* 8: 27–48.

Osgood, A. K., and R. D. Schroeder. Forthcoming. Public assistance receipt: A comparison of black and white single-father families.

Oyserman, D., M. Kemmelmeier, S. Fryberg, H. Brosh, and T. Hart-Johnson. 2003. Racial-ethnic self schemas. *Social Psychology Quarterly* 66: 333–47.

Parke, R. 1995. Fathers and families. In *Handbook of parenting*, vol. 3, ed. M. Bornstein. Mahwah, NJ: Lawrence Erlbaum.

Peters, M. F. 1985. Racial socialization of young black children. In *Black children: Social, educational and parental environments*, ed. H. P. McAdoo and J. L. McAdoo, 159–73). Beverly Hills, CA: Sage.

Phinney, J. S., and V. Chavira. 1995. Parental ethnic socialization and adolescent coping with problems related to ethnicity. *Journal of Research on Adolescence* 5(1): 31–53.

Pirog-Good, M. A. 1993. In-kind contributions as child support: The teen alternative parenting program. In *Young unwed fathers: Changing roles and emerging policies*, ed. R. Lerman and T. Ooms, 251–66. Philadelphia: Temple University Press.

Plechaty, M., S. Couturier, M. Cote, M-A. Roy, J. Massicotte, and M-H. Freeston. 1996. Dimensional analysis of past and present satisfaction in relation to present marital satisfaction. *Psychological Reports* 78(2): 657–58.

Plotnick, R. D., I. Garfinkel, S. S. McLanahan, and I. Ku. 2004. Better child support enforcement: Can it reduce teenage premarital childbearing? *Journal of Family Issues* 25(5): 634–57.

Polkinghorne, D. E. 1988. *Narrative knowing and the human sciences.* Albany: State University of New York Press.

Primus, W. 2006. Improving public policies to increase the income and employment of low-income nonresident fathers. In *Black males left behind*, ed. R. B. Mincy, 211–48. Washington, DC: The Urban Institute Press.

Reich, J. A. 2005. *Fixing families: Parents, power, and the child welfare system.* New York: Routledge.

Risman, B. J. 1986. Can men "mother"? Life as a single father. *Family Relations* 35(1): 95–102.

Rivara, F., P. Sweeney, and B. Henderson. 1986. Black teenage fathers: What happens when the child is born? *Pediatrics* 78: 151–58.

Rivara, F., P. Sweeney, and B. Henderson. 1987. Risk of fatherhood among black teenage males. *American Journal of Public Health* 77: 203–5.

Robinson, B. E. 1988. *Teenage fathers.* Lexington, MA: Lexington Books.

Robinson, B. E., and R. L. Barrett. 1986. *The developing father: Emerging roles in contemporary society.* New York: Guilford Press.

Roy, K. 1999. Low-income single fathers in an African American community and the requirements of welfare reform. *Journal of Family Issues* 20(4): 432–57.

Russell, G., and N. Radin. 1983. Increased paternal participation: The fathers' perspectives. In *Fatherhood and family policy*, ed. M. Lamb and A. Sagi, 139–65. Hillsdale, NJ: Lawrence Erlbaum.

Sampson, R. J., S. W. Raudenbush, and F. Earls. 1997. Neighborhoods and violent crime: A multilevel study of collective efficacy. *Science* 277: 918–24.

Sanders-Thompson, F. L. 1994. Socialization to race and its relationship to racial identification among African Americans. *Journal of Black Psychology* 20(2): 175–88.

Santrock, J. W., and R. A. Warshak. 1979. Father custody and social development in boys and girls. *Journal of Social Issues* 35(4): 112–25.

Savage, B. D. 1987. *Child support and teen parents.* Washington, DC: Adolescent Prevention Clearinghouse, Children's Defense Fund.

Seltzer, J. 1991. Relationships between fathers and children who live apart: The Father's role after separation. *Journal of Marriage and the Family* 53 (February): 79–101.

Scheffler, T. S., and P. J. Naus. 1999. The relationship between fatherly affirmation and a woman's self-esteem, fear of intimacy, comfort with womanhood and comfort with sexuality. *The Canadian Journal of Human Sexuality* 8(1): 39–45.

Schroeder, E. 2008. Is it ever appropriate to spank a child? Issue summary. In *Taking sides: Clashing views in family and personal relationships*, 7th ed. New York: McGraw Hill Contemporary Learning Series.

Scott, L. D., Jr. 2003. The relation of racial identity and racial socialization to coping with discrimination among African American adolescents. *Journal of Black Studies* 33(4): 520–38.

Smith, C. A., M. D. Krohn, R. Chu, and O. Best. 2005. African American fathers: Myths and realities about their involvement with their firstborn children. *Journal of Family Issues* 26(7): 975–1001.

Smith, R. M., and C. W. Smith. 1981. Child rearing and single-parent fathers. *Family Relations* 30(3): 411–17.

Snarey, J. 1993. *How fathers care for the next generation: A four-decade study.* Cambridge, MA: Harvard University Press.

Sonenstein, F. L., J. H. Pleck, and L. Ku. 1991. Levels of sexual activity among adolescent males, *Family Planning Perspectives* 23(4): 162–67.

South, S. J. 1993. Racial and ethnic differences in the desire to marry. *Journal of Marriage and Family* 55(2): 357–70.

Spencer, M. B. 1983. Children's cultural values and parental child rearing strategies. *Developmental Review* 3: 351–70.

Starrels, M. E. 1994. Gender differences in parent-child relations. *Journal of Family Issues* 15(1): 148–65.

Steinberg, L., and S. B. Silverberg. 1987. Influences on marital satisfaction during the middle stages of the family life cycle. *Journal of Marriage and the Family* 49 (November): 751–60.

Stevenson, H. C., Jr. 1994. Validation of the scale of racial socialization for black adolescents: Steps toward multidimensionality. *Journal of Black Psychology* 20(4): 445–68.

Stevenson, H. C., Jr. 1995. Relationship of adolescent perceptions of racial socialization to racial identity. *Journal of Black Psychology* 21: 49–70.

Stier, H., and M. Tienda. 1993. Are men marginal to the family? Insights from Chicago's inner city. In *Men, work and family*, ed. J. C. Hood. Newbury Park, CA: Sage.

Taylor, R., L. Chatters, M. B. Tucker, and E. Lewis. 1990. Developments in research on black families: A decade review. *Journal of Marriage and the Family* 52 (November): 993–1014.

Taylor, R. J., B. R. Leashore, and S. Toliver. 1988. An assessment of the provider role as perceived by black males. *Family Relations* 37(4): 426–31.

Tedder, S. L., K. M. Libbee, and A. Scherman. 1981. A community support group for single custodial fathers. *Personnel and Guidance Journal* 60: 115–19.

Testa, M., N. Astone, M. Krogh, and K. Neckerman. 1989. Ethnic variation in employment and marriage among inner-city fathers. *The Annals of the American Academy of Political and Social Science* 501: 79–91.

Thornton, M. C., L. M. Chatters, R. J. Taylor, and W. R. Allen. 1990. Sociodemographic and environmental correlates of racial socialization by black parents. Special issue: Minority children. *Child Development* 61(2): 401–9.

Tucker, B. M., and C. Mitchel-Kernan, eds. 1995. *The decline in marriage among African Americans: Causes, consequences, and policy implications.* New York: Russell Sage Foundation.

U.S. Census Bureau. 2000. Summary File 2, Matrices PCT8, PCT17, PCT18, PCT26, PCT27, and PCT28. Available from http://factfinder.census.gov/servlet/QTTable?_bm=y&-geo_id=01000US&-qr_name=DEC_2000_SF2_U_QTP10&-ds_name=DEC_2000_SF2_U&-reg=DEC_2000_SF2_U_QTP10: 001 | 451 | 453&-_lang=en&-redoLog=false.

U.S. Census Bureau. 2003. *Statistical abstract of the United States* [Electronic version]. Available from www.census.gov/prod/www/statistical-abstract-us.html.

U.S. Census Bureau. 2004. *Living arrangements of children under 18 years old: 1960 to present.* Table CH.1 [Electronic version]. Available from www.census.gov/population/www/socdemo/hh-fam.html.

U.S. Census Bureau. 2007a. *Current population survey, annual social and conomic supplements.* Table F-22. Married-couple families with wives' earnings greater than husbands' earnings: 1981 to 2005 (selected years). Available from www.census.gov/hhes/www/income/histinc/f22.html.

U.S. Census Bureau. 2007b. Living arrangements of children under 18 years/1 and marital status of parents, by age, sex, race, and Hispanic origin/2 and selected characteristics of the child for all children 2006. Black alone. Table C.3 [Electronic version]. Available from www.census.gov/population/www/socdemo/hh-fam/cps 2006.html.

U.S. Census Bureau. 2007c. Living arrangements of children under 18 years/1 and marital status of parents, by age, sex, race, and Hispanic origin/2 and selected characteristics of the children for all children: 2006. White alone [Electronic version] Table C.3. Available from www.census.gov/population/www/socdemo/hh-fam/cps2006.html

Updegraff, K. A., S. M. McHale, A. C. Crouter, and K. Kupanoff. 2001. Parents' involvement in adolescents' peer relationships: A comparison of mothers' and fathers' roles. *Journal of Marriage and Family* 63(3): 655–68.

Videon, T. M. 2005. Parent-child relations and children's psychological well-being: Do dads matter? *Journal of Family Issues* 26(1): 55–78.

Waller, M. R., and R. Swisher. 2006. Fathers' risk factors in fragile families: Implications for "healthy" relationships and father involvement. *Social Problems* 53(3): 392–420.

Wattenberg, E. 1993. Paternity actions and young fathers. In *Young unwed fathers: Changing roles and emerging policies*, ed. R. Lerman and T. Ooms, 213–34. Philadelphia: Temple University Press.

Wherry, L., and K. Finegold, K. 2004. Marriage promotion and the living arrangements of black, Hispanic, and white children. New Federalism. Series B. No. B-61, (September). The Urban Institute. http://newfederalism.urban.org.

Wille, D. E. 1995. The 1990s: Gender differences in parenting roles. *Sex Roles* 33: 803–17.

Williams, C. L. 1992. The glass elevator: Hidden advantages for men in the "female" professions. *Social Problems* 39(3): 253–67.

Wilson, W. J. 1987. *The truly disadvantaged*. Chicago: Chicago University Press.

Winkler, E. N. 2008. "It's like arming them": African American mothers' views on racial socialization. In *The changing landscape of work and family in the American middle class: Reports from the field*, ed. E. Rudd and L. Descartes, 211–41. Lanham, MD: Lexington Books.

Youniss, J., and J. Smollar. 1985. Adolescent relations with mothers, fathers, and friends. Chicago: University of Chicago Press.

Zarit, S. H., and D. J. Eggebeen. 1995. Parent-child relationships in adulthood and old age. In *Handbook of parenting*, vol. 1, ed. M. Bornstein. Hillsdale, NJ: Lawrence Erlbaum.

Zavodny, M. 1999. Determinants of recent immigrants' locational choices. *International Migration Review* 33(4): 1014–30.

Zeleny, J. 2008. Jesse Jackson apologizes for remarks on Obama. *New York Times*, July 10. Online at www.nytimes.com/2008/07/10/us/politics/10jackson.html?ex+1216353600&en=972&oref=slogin.

Index

About the Author

Roberta L. Coles received her PhD in sociology from the University of Wisconsin at Madison. She has been on the faculty in the Department of Social and Cultural Sciences at Marquette University since 1995, where she teaches courses on family, race and family, race and ethnic relations, and social inequality. Her family-related research has been published in the *Journal of Aging Studies*, *Journal of Contemporary Ethnography*, *Families in Society*, *Journal of African American Men*, and the *Western Journal of Black Studies*.